T0357033

FROM THE REZ
TO THE RUNWAY

ALSO BY CHRISTIAN ALLAIRE

The Power of Style: How Fashion and Beauty
Are Being Used to Reclaim Cultures

FROM THE REZ TO THE RUNWAY

FORGING MY PATH IN FASHION

A MEMOIR

CHRISTIAN ALLAIRE

Collins

An imprint of HarperCollins Publishers Ltd

Published by Collins, an imprint of HarperCollins Publishers Ltd

FIRST EDITION

HarperCollins books may be purchased for educational, business, or sales promotional use through our Special Markets Department.

HarperCollins Publishers Ltd
Bay Adelaide Centre, East Tower
22 Adelaide Street West, 41st Floor
Toronto, Ontario, Canada
M5H 4E3

www.harpercollins.ca

Library and Archives Canada Cataloguing in Publication
Title: From the rez to the runway : forging my path
in fashion : a memoir / Christian Allaire.
Names: Allaire, Christian, 1992- author.
Identifiers: Canadiana (print) 20240522427 | Canadiana (ebook) 20240523768 | ISBN 9781443470629 (softcover) | ISBN 9781443470636 (Ebook)
Subjects: LCSH: Allaire, Christian, 1992- | LCSH: Fashion editors—Canada—Biography. | LCSH: Fashion editors—Nipissing First Nation—Biography. | CSH: First Nations journalists—Nipissing First Nation—Biography. | CSH: Ojibway—Nipissing First Nation—Biography. | LCGFT: Autobiographies.
Classification: LCC TT505.A45 A3 2025 | DDC 070.4/4974692092—dc23

Printed and bound in the United States of America
25 26 27 28 29 LBC 5 4 3 2 1

For all the little rez kids with a dream

FOREWORD

BY JEANNE BEKER

WHEN I BEGAN hosting *Fashion Television* in the mid-eighties, fashion was entering a golden age, about to explode into a glorious mash-up of unprecedented creativity, with a dazzling cast of players promoting unbridled self-expression. Designers were becoming the new rock stars, and the models were their muses, resulting in some sensational sartorial imagery that set new standards for the shape of things to come. It all made for a wildly colourful, electric arena that was a wonderland of unlimited possibilities, and it's no surprise that what our cameras managed to capture over the next twenty-seven years provided endless fantasy fare for fashion fans around the world.

Sometimes, I felt a little guilty for perhaps overhyping the scene: an entire generation of style aficionados was encouraged to get into the business because of the window *Fashion Television* opened onto that ultra-glam world. And as most people now realize, this business is not for the faint of heart: it can be as tough and ruthless as it is exciting and enriching. Still, we'd opened a Pandora's box. Little did I know just how much of an impact our show would have on one particular young Ojibwe teen growing up on the Nipissing First Nation reserve—a young man who was inspired not only to follow his dreams but to pursue a career in fashion that would help edify and empower so many others.

While Indigenous creators had always been amazing artisans when it came to cultural and sartorial expression, precious few had ever managed to receive the attention of the fashion cognoscenti they so deserved. The masterful work of Indigenous designers was a buried treasure waiting to be unearthed, and Christian Allaire was eager to expose it.

The first time I remember taking note of his byline was in 2018, when he wrote a powerful piece for *Vogue* about six Indigenous designers who were reclaiming their heritage, and how my hometown of Toronto was about to host its first Indigenous Fashion Week. Shortly afterwards, I caught wind of the fact that Christian was a fellow Canadian, and when I read a feature on him in the *Toronto Star* in 2020 calling him "a new kind of Vogue editor," I was buoyed to think that this young talent from Ontario was not only making his mark on the esteemed pages of *Vogue* magazine, but was also telling the kinds of game-changing fashion stories that needed to be heard. I began following him and, before long, fell in love with his spirited sense of personal style, keen eye, and wonderful way of writing.

In 2022, ten years after *Fashion Television* had gone off the air, Christian asked if he could interview me for *Vogue*. I was both delighted and honoured. But what was especially moving for me was hearing how influential *Fashion Television* had been for him. "I was raised on that show!" he laughed. As it had done for so many kids growing up in small towns across Canada and around the world—kids who sometimes felt isolated, as though they weren't represented or didn't belong—our series had planted untold seeds that grew into big dreams. And since Christian was not merely a dreamer but a doer, he made up his mind that he was going to somehow make his big fashion dreams come true.

I came away from my interview with Christian feeling incredibly inspired: Here was the next generation, the hope for fashion's future, adamant about telling stories and giving rising new talents a voice. The torch had been passed. And Christian was carrying it with incomparable aplomb.

FROM THE REZ
TO THE RUNWAY

MAADKAMGAD
(THE BEGINNING)

THE STEADY BEAT of the powwow drum—a hypnotic sound that always reminds me of home—slowly crescendos as the models begin to walk. The lights go up; people in their seats hush up and sit up straight. One by one, various Indigenous beauties appear on the long, raised catwalk and proceed to strut. Shutters click at rapid-fire speeds at the end of the runway, where the photographer's pit is capturing every ensemble—a chaotic sound that only adds to the growing excitement of the room.

It's 2019, and it's the Santa Fe Indian Market down in New Mexico. At the annual market, Indigenous artists from across North America take over the downtown plaza in Santa Fe to set up booths and sell their work—whether that be pottery, jewellery, textile, or clothing. For many of the artists, a significant portion of their yearly income is made here. The annual

3

Indigenous Fashion Show is also a standout event at the market, where North America's leading Indigenous designers present their new ready-to-wear collections. I've got a front-row seat for all of the action, of course. I'm here covering the market and fashion show for *Vogue* magazine, where I'm currently the fashion and style writer.

It's my first time attending the Indigenous Fashion Show, which is praised as *the* fashion show for Indigenous designers. I quickly realize why this is the case. The diverse array of designers in the presentation that follows—who span a variety of tribal nations, locations, and styles—perfectly exemplifies the vast beauty found within Indigenous culture. Some of the models are adorned in striking traditional pieces, like Margaret Roach Wheeler's hand-woven dresses; others rock more contemporary wears, like Lesley Hampton's glitzy evening gowns. As I take in each look coming down the runway, it becomes apparent why the show draws such a jam-packed audience every year: It powerfully proves that we as Native people are not monochrome—that we do not all look or dress the same. Also, the outfits are just flat-out gorgeous.

I'm Ojibwe and I grew up on the Nipissing First Nation, a reserve located in northern Ontario, Canada. I've been exposed to such fabulous Native fashions since I was born. My older sister, Alysha, is a jingle dress dancer, and our family often went out to our community's summer powwows to watch her dance. Some of my earliest memories of falling in love with fashion happened at these very powwows. I always loved watching my sister slip into her jingle dress, which is adorned with beautiful ribbons and metal cones and makes a lovely little jingle with each step. I would also gaze at the more elaborate powwow regalia that some of my cousins would wear—like the male fancy dancers, who often sport elaborate porcupine hair roach headpieces, which are often shaped into a mohawk style.

From a young age, I always knew that what we wore—and what our garments signified—was important to our people. Our regalia has never been about just the aesthetics (though they are, indeed, beautiful). They signify a passing-down of traditions, and a maintaining of cultural pride. At the Santa Fe show, as I watched some of North America's most talented Indigenous designers showcasing their work, this idea resonated with me even more. Despite years of oppression and government attempts to strip our people of our cultural practices, the striking fashion show proves that *we are still here*—and in fact thriving—creating some of the most beautiful clothes you've ever seen, despite the odds.

As I'm watching the models do their most dramatic walks and twirls in the garments on the catwalk, I briefly look down at my own ensemble—and I immediately feel a sense of shame over what *I'm* wearing. I realize that I'm not wearing, and nor do I own, a single piece of Native-made *anything*: not my shoes, not my shirt, and certainly not the cheap jewellery I got for five dollars from a street vendor in Chinatown. I look at the crowd around me, and I notice everyone else in the front row is decked out in Indigenous fashion pieces. The couture-level outfits—whether it be the long dentalium shell earrings or the floral-print Jamie Okuma dresses—are almost as good as the ones on the damn catwalk! I can feel my face get hot with embarrassment. *Bro, are you even Native?* I ask myself.

Once the show comes to an end, and the designers have all taken their bows at the end of the runway, the room instantly buzzes with excitement. I eavesdrop on the wealthy fashion collectors, who are already sharing which looks they're going to immediately pre-order. I overhear some Native fashionistas snarkily gossip about which designs they loved, and which they hated. But, again, I can't really hear anything clearly—because I'm too busy looking at what everyone is wearing. There's a sense of cultural flair that permeates the room. It doesn't matter if you're wearing Prada or Gucci here—great style is measured in which Native designer you're wearing, or which family member made your custom earrings. It's a place where boujee Natives can truly shine.

Growing up, I always struggled with my Native identity. I rarely embraced any sense of Indigenous style, like my sister did with her beautiful jingle dresses. My mother is Ojibwe, and my father is French Canadian and Italian. I inherited Dad's fair complexion, so all my life, I've been told I don't "look Native." This created a sense of shame and confusion in me as a kid— so much so that I began believing it myself and shunned my Indigenous side. As a teen, I would have rather been *caught dead* than wear our Ojibwe culture's traditional ribbon shirts. I went through virtually every fashion phase trying to find myself, though—whether it be embracing my preppy side or going completely punk-goth. (Both of which were unfortunate fashion phases for me—my parents don't even have photos of me from this time period in their beloved photo albums!)

My inability to embrace my Indigenous culture—and my desire to shun Indigenous fashion altogether—stemmed from the lack of Native representation in mainstream magazines and television. I certainly didn't see Indigenous culture or fashion in *Vogue*, where I work now. But in Santa Fe, after seeing my fellow Native folks completely *decked out*, something clicked inside of me. Though I looked perfectly stylish on paper in my black suit, tie-dye tee, and heeled boots, I felt something I rarely ever felt: Completely underdressed. Foolish, even.

Call it an *aha* moment, but attending that fashion show was a cultural awakening; it inspired me to reclaim a part of myself that I had suppressed for so many years. Fashion, I realized, could be more than just what you wear: it could be a tool to reconnect with yourself. And boy, did I have a lot of shopping to do.

CHAPTER 1

BEKNAAGED MSHKAWENDAM (WINNER'S DETERMINATION)

IT WAS HER AGAINST ME. And there could only be one winner.

My sister Alysha and I were about to compete in our recurring "fashion show" contest. It's a game that our cousins Jade and Cassidy would make us play whenever they babysat us at our parents' house. How and *why* they came up with this game, I still don't know, but it wasn't the only peculiar one they had us take part in. (Another classic competition was called "Dead Horses," where the task was to see who could "play dead," by lying on the floor, silent and unmoving, the longest. I now realize it was just a clever way to make me and my sister shut up for a good hour or so.)

But back to the fashion show contest.

The rules were quite simple: Alysha and I would have ten minutes to come up with a show-stopping catwalk look—the caveat being that it had to be made using only found objects from around the house. Towels, brooms, clothes, pillows: nothing was off limits in order to make our couture creations come to life. Once we had our final look, my sister and I would then have to "walk the runway" donning the handmade ensemble in front of our cousins, who would judge both of the looks and determine the grand winner. Only one look would come out on top. But the DIY'd garment wasn't the only thing being judged—you had to really *sell it*, too.

I took the competition very seriously. I've been extremely competitive since birth. I hate losing; it simply isn't an option for me. I am, by all means, a sore loser. Besides, my sister was already starting to excel at both sports *and* school. Fashion and the arts was supposed to be *my* thing. And I'd be damned before I let her win this competition, too.

"The timer starts now!" Jade yelled from the kitchen.

"Ready, set, *fashion!*"

With only ten minutes on the clock, my sister and I bolted around the house in search of the very best props to complete our outfits. Adrenaline pumped through my veins. My heart beat at a furious rate, like I was running on a treadmill at full speed.

My sister and I both ran upstairs to our mom's closet. I knew exactly what I wanted. "I saw it first!" I screamed angrily as we both reached for one of our mom's fur coats, which she never wore. With ferocity, I yanked it off the closet hanger as my sister tried to snatch it out of my hands. "*It's mine!*" I won the tug-of-wear and ran off down the hallway, the plushy fur coat piled up in my arms.

I instantly had a vision about using the coat as an Old Hollywood–style shrug. It would make whatever outfit I wore underneath it appear luxurious and expensive. But still, I needed an under layer. *Think, Christian, think!* I ran downstairs towards the kitchen, and tried to come up with something more creative and unexpected to wear.

Aha!

I yanked open the cabinet under the kitchen sink and retrieved a large box of black garbage bags. You know—the big, shiny kind. I had the genius idea of transforming one into a strapless, latex-like minidress. This was, obviously, inspired by Posh Spice—my style icon at the time—who wore a similar frock in the *Spice World* movie.

I got to work, haphazardly wrapping the garbage bag around myself, somehow transforming it into a saucy little tube dress. Voila, I had the perfect little black dress. I then shrugged the fur coat over one shoulder, like I was Joan Collins. The look was really coming together. But, I wasn't done just yet. I still needed accessories.

"Three minutes left!"

I began to panic. *Shit, I need jewellery.* I ran back upstairs to my mom's room, cursing each step I had to take, losing valuable time, in pursuit of the perfect jewels. As I ascended the long staircase, my sister ran down quickly in the opposite direction and I caught a glimpse of her outfit. From what I could gather, she had decided to go the sportier route: she had fashioned one of my dad's Maple Leaf jerseys into a one-shouldered dress, and she had a fanny pack styled cross-body overtop it. It was half hockey, half haute couture.

She thinks she can beat me in that? I scoffed. *Pshh. I've got this in the bag.*

Back in my parents' room, I scavenged my mom's jewellery box and began layering some of her necklaces. Pearls, silver, gold—I piled it all on. I still needed shoes. All of her heels were much too large for me, so I settled on a pair of her black tights, to keep the look monochromatic and sleek. Plus, it kind of looked like I was wearing over-the-knee boots, if you really squinted. I took a look at myself in her full-length mirror. In the finished ensemble, I felt elegant—like I was worthy of going to the Oscars.

"Time's up!" Jade screamed from downstairs. "Time to walk the runway!"

I took a deep breath. This was my moment to shine.

And, in the words of the great RuPaul, I thought to myself: *Don't fuck it up.*

The runway stage was set.

My cousins fashioned the long main-floor hallway connecting our kitchen, dining room, and living room into a makeshift catwalk. Along the length of it, they set up lamps, flashlights, and anything that emitted some sort of light. Then they turned all the other house lights down low, making the hallway feel dramatic and spotlit. At the very end of the catwalk, Jade and Cassidy sat in two chairs—*thrones*—which gave them a great vantage point from which to judge our looks as we sauntered towards them. Listen, it wasn't a Paris couture show, but for small-town Nipissing, it was a pretty decent setup.

Before my sister and I were to face off on the catwalk, the

tradition was to first choose our "strutting song." This would be an upbeat track that would play as we walked down the runway and tried to sell our look. As kids of the nineties, my sister chose "Everybody (Backstreet's Back)" by the Backstreet Boys; I chose Britney Spears's "Oops! . . . I Did It Again." I *loved* Britney.

It was showtime, baby.

My sister was up first. The music blared from our living room stereo. I heard "Backstreet's back, alright!" and watched her from our staircase, off to the side of the runway. Her final look was, admittedly, strong. Her hockey-jersey dress and fanny pack were punctuated with a pair of my mom's old heels—a shocking accessory to see Alysha in, given she was a true tomboy and detested anything girly. In her hands, she also held a mini hockey stick, making campy swish-swish movements with it as she walked slowly down the hall, as if she were on ice. It was all so theatrical. My cousins hollered in delight, clapping as she did a twirl and made her way back to the kitchen.

Shit. I really had to bring my A game.

I had yet to lose a fashion competition. The game had become *my* game, and now, seeing my sister step it up with a look that was so genius, I felt threatened. But there was no time to stress about it: Britney was already cueing up on the radio.

"Are you ready, Christian," my cousin Cassidy shouted as I took my spot on the runway.

"I was born ready!" I screamed back, exuding false confidence.

The heavy beat of "Oops! . . . I Did It Again" began to wail. I sauntered down the runway fiercely, stroking the fur coat like it was the most luxurious item you'd ever seen. In my hand, I held a long white straw that I fake-smoked like a cigarette. Mid-runway, I did a slow twirl, just the way I saw the nineties models like Shalom Harlow do on *Fashion Television*.

I dropped the fur coat to the ground—discarding it like I owned a hundred thousand other minks.

My cousins clapped and cheered. *Okay*, I thought, *I'm off to a good start.*

As I approached the end of the runway, I could see my cousins' faces more clearly. *They were eating the look up.* My garbage-bag tube dress was clinging to my skin so tightly, but I sucked in extra hard, making sure it clung to all the right places. As I sauntered down to the end of the runway, I caught a glimpse of my sister watching me from the staircase. I blew her an over-the-top kiss. In response, she stuck her tongue out at me and gave me the finger.

It was now time for the judging to begin.

After each fashion competition, my cousins would make my sister and I wait in the living room—still fully dressed—while they secretly deliberated in the kitchen. Alysha and I would often get into fights while we waited, talking shit to each other like siblings do. This time, however, we waited quietly and patiently. For the first time, it felt like there wasn't a clear winner. *Is my sister about to beat me at my own game?*

My cousins finally emerged looking stoic. They loved to act like they were judges on a reality show or something, making the game tense and suspenseful.

"We've thought long and hard," Jade began. "But, as always, there can only be one winner. There are no ties in fashion."

I fidgeted nervously with my mom's heavy necklaces.

"Tonight's winner brought the right mix of layers, fabrics, and performance," Cassidy continued. "They also incorporated unexpected elements that made their outfit shine."

I knew they had to be talking about me. I'd fashioned a god-damn garbage bag into a dress!

"So, the winner is," they said simultaneously, before dramatically pausing.

I braced myself to walk up and accept the winner's trophy, which was just a bunch of silver tinfoil shaped into an Oscars-like statuette. *That was a close match*, I thought.

"ALYSHA!"

It took me a few seconds to realize what I had just heard.

My sister hollered and ran around the room with her trophy—shoving her victory in my face over and over and over. It was the first time I had ever lost a fashion competition. I could feel my face burning up, my cheeks turning a vibrant shade of fire hydrant red. I was completely fucking pissed. How could they pick her dumb outfit over mine?

I began to cry.

Not like a misty little tear; I began to sob.

"I HATE ALL OF YOU!" I screamed.

I stormed out the front door, furiously ripping off my mom's necklaces and discarding them around the front yard. I then tore myself out of my garbage-bag dress—emerging out of it like the Hulk, left only in my little gym shorts and black tights.

It was getting dark out, but I didn't care. I was going to leave home for good and never come back. *I will show them*, I thought as I began walking down our long muddy road with no shoes on. I could hear the distant yelling of my cousins, begging me to come back inside. They were babysitting me, after all—and this baby was fleeing from home.

Fashion meant everything to me. It was my biggest obsession, one of my few interests, and it angered me that my cousins wouldn't even give me *that*. My sister had the book smarts, was outgoing, and had the most friends. She didn't need (or obsess) about fashion like I did. I was the artsy, cool fashion kid, not her. And my cousins had robbed me of that. Good riddance, then!

I wiped away tears as I walked barefoot through our neighbour's yard. I wanted to move out of this dumb town—away from the stupid muddy roads and the stupid babysitter games that I was forced to play. I wanted to move to the glitz and glamour of New York or Paris or London, or one of those other fashion capitals that I'd always read about in *Vogue* or seen on *Fashion Television*. I knew *real* fashion people would appreciate my eye for style. And maybe I would finally fit in. I'd finally be understood.

As I neared the end of our long dirt road, I took a look around. There wasn't a person or approaching car in sight. It was getting really dark now, and I was a little hungry.

Usually, we'd conclude our fashion show contest with a pizza party. I craved a slice of pepperoni-and-cheese real bad. So, I turned around and slowly began to walk back home, picking up the scraps of my dress and my mom's strewn-about necklaces in the front yard. I'd "run away" for about fifteen minutes.

As I came back inside, my cousins and sister tried not to

acknowledge my temper tantrum. I sniffled, but my tears had already dried up.

"We just ordered pizza," Jade said kindly. "You in?"

"Yes, please," I said quietly, as I threw my shredded garbage-bag dress in the trash.

CHAPTER 2

MINO-BIISKONYEWIN
(FASHIONABLY DRESSED)

IT WAS A RARE HOT *and* humid day. Our rez never got this hot—even at the height of summer. This meant one thing: it was time to go swimming.

To make the most of the sweltering day, my mom took my sister and me to our grandma Leda's house, where we often swam in the July and August months when we weren't in school. Grandma's house was located in Garden Village, a small subdivision of Nipissing First Nation—our traditional home-lands, where we spent all of our summers when we were grow-ing up. As kids, her house was our version of heaven, mostly because her backyard opened up onto a picturesque portion of Lake Nipissing, giving us our own little private beach for the entire summer break.

Heading to Grandma's house was always an *event*. We

weren't just going to take advantage of a dip in the lake. A visit to Grandma Leda's meant that we would also be seeing everyone from my mom's side of the family, who all treated the house as a meeting point. And boy, there was always a lot of family to visit with: my mom is one of eighteen children, and all my aunts and uncles each had kids of their own, too, so the house was always chock full of cousins. It was basically like a big, Native version of the Brady Bunch.

In the summers, especially on Sundays, you'd find the whole family gathering for a big rezzy breakfast. In her tiny (but mighty) kitchen, my grandma would usually be baking up a huge pot of beans, or my auntie Joanne would be frying up her famous fry bread (the best ever). Sometimes, the house was so full of people that the kids would have to eat breakfast on the floor, or outside on the grass. The kids never minded, though—in fact, we preferred having time away from the nagging adults.

Grandma Leda was the glue that held our family together. She also scared us. A residential school survivor, Grandma Leda had a quiet strength about her. She also spoke mostly Ojibwe, so she was a woman of few words. But even so, she was always the family member that my sister and I looked forward to seeing the most. Because at Grandma's house, you knew you were loved, cared for, and fed. Boy, were we fed.

Mom and Dad's house was located just ten minutes away from Grandma's, so the ride down to Garden Village—"GV," as we called it—was always filled with a lot of anticipation. To get there, you had to drive down a miles-long road past a dilapidated barn, wide-open farm fields filled with dairy cows, and past the famous rez restaurant—a hybrid lunch spot/gas station that always advertised "Fresh Fish! Caught Local!" but the food was famously terrible.

"Mom, are you gonna come swim with us," I asked in the car, fidgeting in the backseat with my bathing suit already on.

"No," she said, "but I'm sure some of your cousins will want to."

My sister and I were both eating a small order of McDonald's fries, which we always begged for on the car ride down.

Driving down to the rez always felt like crossing some sort of invisible border. There was a tangible energy shift once you arrived. My parents lived in town, and our neighbours were mostly upper-middle-class white French Canadians with perfectly manicured lawns and brand new Hondas. But on the rez, the community signs featured words in Ojibwe, and there were smoke shacks and houses selling pickerel, and big pickup trucks parked in the driveways, and open windows with bed sheets being used as curtains. This, to me, felt like home.

We pulled up to Grandma's house, where a ton of cars were parked out front, which meant that most of the family was already there. My sister and I rapidly unbuckled our seats and began hightailing it to the backyard to immediately jump into the lake.

"Hey!" my dad yelled as he put the van in park. "You guys only have an hour to swim. Lysh needs to get ready for the powwow soon."

Later in the afternoon, we would be heading to our annual Nipissing summer powwow—our community's most famous event. It was held in Jocko Point, just a fifteen-minute car ride away (located deeper in the bush), and all of our community members would show up for the traditional dance. Jingle dress dancers, fancy dancers, grass dancers—everyone came to the powwow in their finest regalia, where they would proceed to dance clockwise in a circle as the powwow drummers provided a steady beat. It was a no-alcohol, no-pictures event, of course—a sacred continuation of tradition.

My sister, who started jingle dress dancing when she was young, was going to be dancing in the powwow that afternoon—even in the humid heat. But that was happening later. For now, Lysh and I cared only about nose-diving right into that cool, refreshing water. As we ran full-speed towards the lake and jumped in from the dock, we could hear Grandma Leda yelling out at us, from up at the house.

"NO RUNNING ON THE DOCK!!"

POWWOW REGALIA IS what, I believe, introduced me to the world of fashion and design.

From as early as I can remember, my mom, my aunties, or my grandma Leda were always sewing regalia around the house—regalia being the traditional attire our people wear for ceremonial purposes or powwows, garments rooted in tradition and intention.

Sometimes, a gaggle of my aunties would come over to our parents' house to work on various pieces for my sister. They'd be sitting around the kitchen table with their sewing machines and smokes as they beaded a new pair of moccasins, or appliquéd ribbons onto a skirt. But the most serious sewing happened at Grandma Leda's house—on her extra-long kitchen table that could easily sit twenty people.

Some of my earliest memories revolve around hearing the sound of the jingles. I would watch my mom and aunties hand-sew rows and rows of metal cones, one by one, onto my sister's many jingle dresses; those cones create a wonderful clinking sound when the finished design is worn. The intention of the jingle sounds, according to our traditions, is to provide healing—both for the dancer, and for those watching. I certainly found the sound to be soothing (and still do).

Though I didn't quite comprehend what a jingle dress meant as a kid, I did recognize that it was a special garment, considering that I saw just how much time, attention, and detail was put into every design. I especially loved the rainbow assortment of ribbons and florals on the dresses. It all seemed so fancy.

I, of course, had custom creations that had been made for me, too. Though I wasn't really interested in them. When I was two years old, my grandma Leda sewed me my very first ribbon shirt, designed in classic shades of red, white, yellow, and black—the four colours of our traditional medicine wheel teachings, which reflect living a harmonious life. To me, though, ribbon shirts didn't seem quite as elaborate or striking as jingle dresses; I was more fascinated by the over-the-top embellishments that Lysh's garments got to have. Inexplicably, I also felt a natural pull towards the more feminine silhouette of a dress or skirt; a button-up shirt just seemed so *plain*. So rigid.

As I watched my mom and aunties and grandma work on various regalia pieces, I would sit there quietly and eavesdrop—stealing sips of my mom's tea, which she always let run ice-cold. I would hear them consider the colours being applied onto the garment, the directions of the ribbons, the angles of the cones, or the density of them.

Being surrounded by this idea that design could be something meaningful—something embedded in culture—deepened my fascination with clothing. I understood from the care taken in creating Indigenous outfits that what you wear should represent your individuality in some way—who you are, where you come from. And I inherently knew that fashion was something that you should take pride in.

Clothing, I realized, wasn't just a necessity. What you wear and put on your back every day should mean something. For me, in fact, clothing meant *everything*.

BACK IN GV, my sister and I were drying off from our swim down by the lake.

"Alysha!" my mom yelled out from up at Grandma's house. "Time to get ready!"

The Nipissing powwow would start in just over an hour, so it was time to braid Lysh's hair and get her into her jingle dress for the afternoon dance.

Inside the house, some of my cousins were already getting dressed in their regalia in the living room. It was a colourful calamity of ribbons, feathers, and jingles; I was always amazed that everyone knew whose regalia was whose, considering the room would turn into one big mess of colours and textures and designs and beadwork.

"Bwaaaa, stand still," barked one of my aunties, as she tried to slip beaded cuffs onto one of my cousins. "Ever fidgety, you."

I was too young to show an interest in powwow dancing myself, so I would watch everyone else get dressed from the sidelines. Seeing the outfits come to life was always my favourite part of the whole thing. I didn't care so much about the actual dancing or powwow part. *I just loved the fittings.* Mostly because they allowed me to see my cousins and my sister in a new light. In our day-to-day, they'd be wearing graphic tees and sporty shorts—but in their ornate regalia, everyone looked so regal. Majestic, even.

"Hey, that ribbon's fraying, eh," my auntie Lola said, eyeing my sister in her dress as she came out from one of the bedrooms. Auntie Lola wasted no time—she got out her trusted tiny little scissors and began to clean up the fraying bits. My aunties were eagle-eyed when it came to the outfits. Everything had to look perfect. You'd think they were couturiers or something.

Once everyone got dressed, it was time over to head to the sacred powwow grounds. It was a real sight to see, watching everyone cram into their cars in their voluminous outfits, but watching them pile out was even funnier. Why they never thought to change *at the location* I'll never know. Perhaps they liked to make an entrance. Us Native people are so dramatic.

The summer powwow in Jocko Point was always a well-attended event. It often got so busy that you had to park your car at the last remaining spot at the end of a long dirt road and then walk the rest of the way in. This afternoon looked as jam-packed as ever. *Guess we'll be walking.* The five-minute walk to the grounds always felt like an hour.

"Don't wear your moccasins," my mom said to my sister as we parked and everyone began to get out of the car. She handed her her sandals. "You'll get them dirty on the walk over."

The dance circle was fairly large at this powwow, which meant the organizers were expecting a big turnout. A mish-mash of beach chairs and folding chairs were set up all around it, as families claimed their spots. Luckily, you didn't have to worry about bringing hats or umbrellas or anything to block the sun. The area was perfectly shaded by trees. A perk of having a powwow in the middle of the bush. (Though I always *hated* the porta-potties.)

On the outer perimeter of the powwow circle were vendors selling beaded jewellery, handmade ribbon shirts, and, of course, fry bread—some of the best fry bread you've ever had probably, which you could also get Indian taco–style, *my* favourite. (For non-Native folks, that's a piece of fry bread with chili, cheese, lettuce, and sour cream on top.)

Mom and Dad set up their chairs near some of my uncles and aunties, who were already parked in a prime viewing spot. My regalia-clad cousins and sister all headed over to take their places in the powwow circle for Grand Entry—the kickoff dance circle. I always felt a little left out when they'd head off, leaving me alone with the adults.

I slumped into a chair and pulled out my pink Game Boy, ready to play *Pokémon*. In retrospect, I had the most terrible attitude at powwows. I would count the seconds until it was over, wishing I was back at home so I could watch *Spice World* or play my Nintendo. I was far too young and naive to recognize the true special beauty of a powwow ceremony. To me, it seemed like just another family function that I was forced to attend.

As everyone began to dance in a circle, I dreamed of being somewhere entirely else.

IT WASN'T JUST my culture's intricate regalia that compelled my interest in the world of style. As I kid, I quickly became interested in fashion from the outside world, too.

It began with the copies of *Vogue* that my mom would, on

occasion, leave strewn around the house. When I was bored, I'd flip through the magazine's glossy pages and take great delight in the editorial spreads, shot by iconic photographers like Steven Meisel or Annie Leibovitz. Poring over these photos transported me to another world—a world where the clothes were otherworldly and totally jaw-dropping.

If our Indigenous clothing taught me that fashion can be deeply personal and reflective of your roots, then the exquisite fashions in *Vogue* taught me that fashion can also be aspirational—even unattainable. I never knew that clothes could be so beautiful and *expensive* until I saw the dreamy couture frocks modelled in *Vogue*. There were beaded and sequined gowns; big fur coats; sky-high stiletto heels; lavish diamond jewellery. None of it looked like anything I'd ever seen on the rez.

I was—one word—*obsessed*.

When my mom wasn't looking, I began to steal her copies of *Vogue* and stash them in my bedroom closet (I still have a pile to this day, in the same closet). At night, just before bed, I would often revisit the pages of these issues, many of which reflected the fashions in the early 2000s. I made a point of folding the corner of the pages where I particularly loved a design or image, bookmarking it for future viewing pleasure.

Vogue wasn't the only thing that introduced me to the world of high fashion. On TV, I quickly became infatuated with *Fashion Television*—a half-hour Canadian program hosted by the legendary fashion journalist Jeanne Beker, in which she would report on the latest designers, trends, and fashion shows.

From the second my eyes landed on it, I couldn't get enough. Watching the show introduced me to what was happening on international runways. It's where I learned about some of the greatest working designers in the world—Karl Lagerfeld, Miuccia Prada, Giorgio Armani, Calvin Klein, and Alexander McQueen. I was captivated by their unique points of view and creativity.

I loved *Fashion Television* so much that, when my dad's cable subscription suddenly dropped the network that it aired on, I had a hissy fit. I *begged him* to pay for the channel. He wouldn't. To counter this, I would go over to the house of my grandparents Laura and Lucien, my dad's parents, because I knew they had the channel. There, I would try to catch one of the new episodes or, at the very least, a favourite rerun. Not having easy access to the show only increased my infatuation.

Watching Jeanne Beker taking her viewers backstage at the shows and reporting live from the front lines of the fashion world, I was transfixed by a world that seemed so out of reach. On the rez, we had our cute little powwows and handmade regalia, sure, but these runways, and the extensive collections debuted on them, were *next level*. That's when I came to understand fashion as a genuine art form—a medium in which true creative genius could be expressed. And the best part about it was that it was a type of art that you could touch. *Wear*.

Watching *Fashion Television* religiously, I made a decision: I *wanted* to be a part of that world. I *needed* to be a part of that world.

I wanted to be front row at a fashion show in New York or Milan or Paris—not at our sweltering powwow in the dead summer heat, sweating my ass off.

I needed to be a part of the glamour.

And I didn't care what it would take for me to get there.

A FEW HOURS into the powwow, the dance circle was finally fizzling out. My sister and cousins were exhausted and hot—their feet were aching from the constant measured steps they'd been taking for hours, always stepping precisely on beat with the drums.

"Hey there, Christian," my aunt Juliette said as she took a seat beside me.

Juliette was like a second mom to my sister and me. She often watched us after school, while we waited for my parents to finish work. She'd feed us cold spaghetti with moose meat in it, or salads with Catalina dressing. Our uncle Pat, meanwhile, would usually be out fishing or hunting. I distinctly recall a dead moose always hanging out in their garage, drying out to be skinned and cut into meat.

I was miserable. My Game Boy battery had died an hour earlier and the mosquitoes were slowly coming out as the sun was beginning to set.

"Hi," I said, dramatically sighing.

"Why don't you ever go out there and dance?" asked Juliette.

I was still very shy, and I mainly didn't want to dance because I didn't want everyone looking at me. I was too self-conscious to dance in front of so many people. But even so, I secretly longed to wear the colourful couture that all my cousins donned.

"I don't know," I moped.

"You know, it's a great honour to dance and to wear our regalia," Juliette continued. "It's what our people have done for centuries. You should really try it sometime!"

If it's so great, I thought to myself, *why have I never seen our powwow regalia in the pages of* Vogue, *or on* Fashion Television?

I felt caught between these two worlds. On one hand, I greatly admired the beauty, storytelling, and craftsmanship that were put into our traditional powwow regalia. But on the other, I rarely saw our cultural designs reflected in the broader fashion world that I was so enamoured by. I'd never seen a jingle dress in *Vogue*, let alone a Native person.

I began to wonder if my Indigenous culture was something to be proud of—or something to be ashamed of. When you don't see something represented in the mainstream, it causes you to doubt its validity. Was our regalia not fashionable? Was it not innovative? I wanted to wear the clothes that were deemed worthy of being on the chic European catwalks. Maybe our Indigenous designs were outdated, a relic of the past.

"Maybe one day I'll dance," I said to my aunt Juliette, hoping she'd leave me alone.

But I had no intention of it. I had already decided that I would soon be crossing over to a different world—a world where the supermodels wore saucy little miniskirts by Donatella Versace, and partied at the Ritz in Paris, and wore cute little monogrammed Louis Vuitton Speedy bags.

And I certainly wouldn't find that in the middle of a bush, while eating my fry bread.

I needed to get off the rez.

CHAPTER 3

SHKADENDMOWIN (GRIEF AND MOURNING TIME)

MY SISTER AND I HAD to be at high school by 8 a.m.

And almost every single day, without fail, I made both of us late. Very late.

Lysh was now in her senior year, and I was two years behind her—a freshman. This morning was no different: I was racing against the clock, rushing to get ready before Dad had to drive us to school. I looked at my alarm clock: I had about five minutes left.

I stood in front of the sliding closet doors in my room, totally paralyzed. I was shirtless, wearing my go-to pair of black skinny jeans and nothing else. I was having a serious outfit crisis—and getting more frustrated by the second. *I have nothing to wear!*

This was, of course, a lie. I had *many* things to wear. My love for fashion and personal style had only snowballed throughout my teen years, and my wardrobe was now bursting along with it. Shopping became my professional hobby. My collection of clothes was pretty much hoarder-level. Each time I dared to slide open my closet, things would come flying out—almost as if they were gasping for air.

I treated getting ready for school like a serious sport. Every morning, I got up extra early to flat iron my naturally curly hair pin-straight—this was the era of Justin Bieber hair, okay!—and to find the perfect outfits to go with "the look," which was often skinny jeans, Converse, and some sort of punky rock-and-roll top with studs or skulls on it. To me, appearance meant everything; I *needed* to put my best foot forward at school.

Usually, I could seamlessly throw an ensemble together—but on this morning, I was seriously lacking style inspiration. I was tired of all my clothes. I furiously rummaged through the hangers to see what I could find, hoping a magical outfit would manifest itself.

I can't wear the McQueen T-shirt, I thought, eyeing the top that I had begged my parents for last Christmas. *I've worn that way too much lately.*

Next, I grabbed a zip-up Diesel hoodie with a big, fuzzy shearling lining on the inside (this was 2008). *I look fat*, I thought as I tried it on, pinching a non-existent roll on the side of my extremely skinny frame.

I wanted a look that was both edgy and chic—like the outfits I saw celebrities and models in the magazines wearing.

"Chris, HURRY UP," Lysh yelled out at me from downstairs. She was sick and tired of my silly style meltdowns that made us late every morning.

"Put on a damn sweater already, fuck!"

I had only two minutes left.

Then I had an *aha* moment.

I remembered the package from the online store SSENSE that had arrived for me just yesterday. It was a black Y-3 cardigan with geometric mesh panels all over it, which made the knitwear look fun and hip. (My parents, for some reason, had indulged me with the purchase—which was on sale.)

I slipped it on over a plain black tee, and kept the go-to skinny jeans in the mix. I finally felt happy with the total look. It was now 8:15 a.m. The deadline was up.

I quickly ran downstairs, aware that my dad and my sister were already waiting for me in the car, which my dad would always keep running—for an added sense of urgency. I headed into the kitchen and, as usual, a warm raspberry Pop-Tart was waiting for me in the toaster. My dad would always leave one out for me, knowing that I'd be running late. I shoved the Pop-Tart in my mouth.

Time for a coat. I threw on my American Eagle parka, which had a cool fur-trimmed hood, and accessorized it with my favourite studded black Y-3 sneakers (clearly, I loved the brand). Strutting out the door to the driveway with my backpack on, I felt stylish in my outfit. Cool. *Famous.* In my sick little head, I even imagined paparazzi snapping photos of me, as I made the five-second walk from the garage to the car.

God, I thought. *I can't go anywhere!*

HIGH SCHOOL WAS—as a whole—pretty uneventful. But I hated going.

The school was in Sturgeon Falls, a town just ten to fifteen minutes off the rez. There were a few Native kids at the school, including my sister and some of my older cousins. But it was a predominantly white school with lots of French-Canadian kids. It was a very small school, and most of my classes had only ten kids or so. Often, fewer.

I didn't have *tons* of friends. But I did have Kasey—my best friend since childhood. Kasey and I got along because, among other things, we both loved fashion. I can say with confidence that we were the best-dressed students in that school. (Sorry, everyone else!)

Dressing up every day for school was definitely my favourite part of the day. This was the late 2000s, so our Y2K style game was always on point. Kasey would wear her best skinny jeans with layered tank tops, finishing off the look with a faux fur–trimmed hoodie from a brand like Aeropostale or American Eagle. I was going through more of a punk-rock phase: I'd wear my black skinny jeans (I even wore women's styles, because they were *tighter*), with checkered Vans slip-on shoes and edgy graphic tees. I'd also pile on black jelly bracelets or studded belts, which I'd often buy from the skater shop West49.

When we finally got to school, Lysh and I immediately went our separate ways. It was the classic sibling trope—we'd never dare to be seen together outside of the house.

Kasey and I had lockers right beside each other, and they were located up on the second floor. We met by our lockers every morning, so while Lysh went her way I headed up the stairs.

I always walked through the school halls quickly, and with a sense of purpose. There were certain kids I tried to avoid seeing.

"Nice pants, fag," said one of those classmates, a popular jock type, just as I reached the second floor. The name-calling didn't faze me much; I was used to it.

I definitely didn't fit in with the other kids in school, who wore sporty logo tees and baggy jeans. I, meanwhile, regularly wore leg warmers as bracelets, or avant-garde jeans all ripped and shredded in a purposeful way. I was often bullied for my eccentric wardrobe. The other kids would call me "gay," or ask why I dressed like a girl.

But I didn't care. I knew I looked good. Their small-town brains just didn't *get it*.

Kasey showed up at the locker in one of her immaculate outfits. She was all in pink today.

"*Okay*, cute coat," I said, as she began to spin her combination.

"Thanks," she said. "I love your shoes!"

Luckily, Kasey and I had the same schedule; today was math, English, science, and gym. I *hated* gym the most. For one, getting all sweaty while playing some godforsaken sport ruined my straightened hair, making it all curly again. Even worse, the boy's locker room gave me major anxiety.

I knew I wasn't like the other boys in school. Overhearing them make crude comments about some of the girls in our class—"Bro, did you see her nipples through her shirt?"—sent a shiver down my spine. The way they punched each other or farted on each other or slapped each other on the ass felt so barbaric. I wanted nothing to do with any of them. Whenever the bell rang and it was time to go to the locker room, I changed out of my gym clothes as quickly as possible so I could get the hell out of there.

I didn't want to admit it, but as much as I was horrified by the other boys in school, I also harboured a bizarre attraction to some of them. And I was ashamed of this. As I changed out of my clothes at rapid speed, I'd sometimes sneak a quick peek at some of their bare chests—all sweaty and chiselled with high-metabolism teenage abs. I knew I was likely gay. But being accused of being gay by the high-school bullies made me convince myself it wasn't true. As I finished getting changed, I avoided eye contact with all of them, and then met up with Kasey outside the gym.

After school, my routine was pretty much set. I walked over to my grandma and grandpa's house on my dad's side—we called them Memère and Pepère—which was a short five-minute walk from the school. My grandpa Lucien, a real French-Canadian man, would sometimes sneak me a drink, like a Caesar with extra vodka. My grandma Laura—who'd immigrated from Fano, Italy, during the war—had a love language of food; she'd always whip me up a snack to tide me over until my dad picked me up after work.

After Dad drove me home, I hightailed it up to my room and instantly logged on to my computer—one of those huge desktop kinds. The internet was my safe space. A place where I could deep-dive into my hobbies and interests without judgment. As a result, I became well-versed in the world of chat rooms.

I logged on to one of my favourite virtual hangouts—it was called Habbo Hotel, a virtual "hotel" where your avatar could chat with fellow "guests"—and saw that a few of my internet friends were online, including Natasha, my favourite.

Natasha and I often direct-messaged (on MSN Messenger!) about fashion. She lived somewhere in rural America, and we both hated the small towns we were growing up in. One of our favourite games was to log onto Style.com (RIP), where we'd pull up a runway show and, look by look, "review" the collections and share our thoughts about them.

"What show should we do today?" I typed.

We pulled up the new Dior collection. It was Paris Fashion Week, so we had fresh content to dissect. "I *love* the shoes in Look 3," Natasha wrote. "I feel like they make everything look expensive."

"The dress silhouette is interesting in Look 5," I wrote back. "It's formal, but not."

We went back and forth, sharing our (naive and uneducated) opinions about all of the expensive looks. I didn't know Natasha—if that was even her real name—but she played a big role in how I dissected fashion and thought about it on a deeper level.

As we browsed all of the collections, I would long to be a part of that world. In school, we were beginning to toy around with the idea of what we wanted to "be" when we were older—and all I knew was that I wanted to be in the front row of those shows. I didn't know exactly what I wanted to do, but I did know that I wanted to work in fashion.

"Chris, supper's ready!"

After dinner, my parents would encourage me to stay off the internet, but I'd usually head right back up to my room and resume reading about celebrities and fashions. When they'd finally kick me off the computer, I'd turn to the pages of the *Vogue* magazines we had lying around the house, or I'd try to watch YouTube clips of *Fashion Television* for the millionth time.

The world of style seemed like it could be my escape out of this crummy town. And soon, my desire to leave and follow my dream into fashion would become a much more urgent call to action.

"HEY. PSST. CHRISTIAN. *Wake up.*"

I couldn't tell if I was asleep or awake, until I felt my mom's warm hand on my shoulder. I turned over in my bed and found her standing over me. Seeing her there startled me.

"What," I said groggily and grumpily, my eyes barely open.

It was still dark out. I was confused.

Is it time for school already?

"We have to tell you something," she said through tears. My dad stood in the doorway.

I sat up slowly, wiping my eyes. Something was wrong. My heart began to beat faster.

My parents stood there in silence for a few seconds. My mom looked at my dad, signalling him to take the lead.

"Robin's dead," my dad said in a monotone, with no emotion on his face.

I thought I had misheard him. Only I hadn't.

"What?" I said.

"Your cousin Robin is dead," my dad said again.

My mom let out a quiet sob.

I lay back down again in total shock.

"What . . . how?" I said. I could feel tears welling up in my eyes. "How?"

Before passing on to the spirit world, Robin had been one of my closest cousins growing up.

As kids, Robin would come over to our house or I'd go to his, and we'd watch movies like *Scream*, *Mortal Kombat*, or anything with Jet Li or Jackie Chan (our favourites). Robin was one of my funniest cousins—a truly silly dude who could make me laugh harder than anyone else—and he had a heart of gold. He had piercing blue eyes that were as kind as he was.

As kids, we were inseparable. But as teens, we began falling out of touch. We didn't go to the same high school, for one, and I didn't quite like the crowd he was hanging out with. I wasn't dumb; I knew that Robin and his friends had started dabbling in drugs.

His death, my parents told me, was ruled an accidental methadone overdose.

Addiction in the community was not uncommon. Many on the rez suffered, and still do suffer, from addiction. It's one of the awful legacies of the cultural annihilation of Indigenous people, who had to endure forced family separations, residential schooling, and relocations onto reservation lands. The intergenerational trauma lingers, passing through bloodlines with relentless ease. The isolation and lack of opportunities on the rez also make it easy to rely on drugs and alcohol as coping mechanisms; for that brief high, no matter how brief, you get to forget all your troubles and all the barriers in front of you.

It was no secret that some of my cousins did drugs. But Robin's overdose was still a shock to the whole family. He was just so *young*. Unfathomably young. For weeks after, I simply couldn't comprehend his death. I had never experienced a loss like this.

That whole morning after I found out was a blur. Despite my grief, I put together the best black mourning outfit I could: a black cardigan with leather patches on the elbows and a pair of dressy black jeans. Through my style, no matter how frivolous it seemed, I wanted to look respectable and honour my cousin.

Mom and Dad drove me and my sister to Grandma's house, to be with the rest of the family. That's what you did in times of crisis in our family—you gathered, even if there was no set agenda or plan. You just *showed up* for each other.

There was no shortage of food there, which was laid out in the kitchen. There was fry bread, beans, salads, macaroni salad, desserts. A big pot of coffee, brewing at all times. If my grandma was going to focus on one thing in our time of grief, it was keeping people fed.

Word spread quickly on the rez, and it didn't take long for local community members to stop by too. Neighbours popped in and out of the house, sharing their brief condolences. Everyone consoled each other through tears.

I don't think I ate a single thing, or said a single word, the whole time I was there. I couldn't bring myself to look at Robin's mom, who was beside herself with grief. It was just too painful. I was sad, but I was also angry—annoyed that nobody seemed to care how I felt. *If anyone should be sad*, I thought to myself as I sat in a corner of the room, *it should be me. Robin and I were the closest of everyone here.*

It also annoyed me that people kept saying, "He was so young—it's *such a waste.*"

I hated that. I didn't see Robin's existence as a waste. In fact, I saw his drug use—and his accidental death—as a way out. It was a way to cope. Life on the rez can make you feel loved and surrounded by your own people, but it can also make you feel stuck. I wasn't angry about his drug use, like so many others in the room. I empathized with it. I understood it. And I remember thinking it could have just as easily been me.

LATER THAT NIGHT, a traditional sacred fire was lit in Robin's honour outside Grandma's house.

In our family, the sacred fire was to be kept burning until the person who had recently died was buried or cremated. This meant the fire might burn for days on end; Firekeepers—some of my older cousins, in a role usually held by men—would sleep in shifts, with someone always by the fire to poke it and make sure it didn't fizzle out.

The purpose of the sacred fire was to help carry someone's soul up to the spirit world. In our culture, it's believed that smoke is a conduit; it helps lift up the spirit and carry it to the place that it belongs. To pay your respects to the deceased, you throw a small piece of cedar or tobacco into the fire and share a few words.

That night, some of the cousins and I sat around the fire. They shared stories about Robin, but I was still too shell-shocked to say anything. But hearing my cousins' stories about him—especially the funny memories—did help to alleviate some of my pain.

"Hey, do you guys remember that time Robin 'dove' off of Joe's Cliff?" my cousin Theo asked as he poked the embers.

Joe's Cliff was an infamous cliff near my grandma's house where we all went to swim in the summer. As kids, the ten-foot drop seemed like it was sixty feet high. We all loved diving off of it—or, sometimes, pushing each other off.

We all laughed. On one occasion, Robin's "dive" off the cliff had turned into a notorious belly flop, which hurt for hours afterwards. Natives *love* to laugh, even in the darkest of times; it's probably our best defence mechanism.

As I watched the flames of the fire intensify, and listened to the soothing crackling of the wood, I began to disappear into my own thoughts.

Robin's passing was a wake-up call for me. I realized that I needed to get serious about my own future. I needed to start thinking about what I wanted to do with my life—and make a plan for how to achieve it.

Up until that moment, the glitzy fashion world I longed to be a part of had been a distant dream, something that seemed so out of reach. Impossible, even. But I knew that staying on the rez wasn't going to make it come true either. I was determined to make my vision come to life, to make something of myself.

I loved rez life—but I also needed to escape it.

And as I shed a silent tear for Robin, hoping nobody would notice, I vowed I would do anything to make my dream come true.

I owed it to kids like Robin, who didn't have the opportunity.

Robin burned fast—but bright—on this earth. And he made me want to shine bright, too.

CHAPTER 4

AANJI-BMAADZIWIN
(BEGIN A NEW LIFE)

WHEN THE DAY CAME THAT I finally left home—my family, our rez, everything I had ever known—I was overcome with a sense of melancholy that I hadn't anticipated.

In my parents' driveway, Mom, Dad, and I finished packing up the car. I had graduated high school just a few months prior, and now, as the summer was coming to a close, I was officially headed to Toronto to pursue my post-secondary studies.

The big city.

"Is everything going to fit?" I asked skeptically, as my dad tried to shove in three suitcases and several bins of clothes. (I *needed* all my clothes, of course.)

"It's *going* to fit," Dad said, disgusted with the excessiveness of it all.

The SUV was packed *to the brim* for our five-hour road trip to Toronto. Mom had gone overboard on the dorm room shopping. I could have outfitted a three-bedroom apartment with the number of furnishings and trinkets and sheets and pillows she bought for my room, which was about the size of a walk-in closet.

Seeing my life packed into the backseat of a car felt bizarre. Sure, I was excited to finally pursue my dreams, and to move to a city where I'd always felt I belonged. But I also felt a foreignness that made me anxious. *Would people like me? What if I missed home?*

Dad finally managed to slam the trunk shut, and our Toronto road trip began.

I was going to study at Ryerson University (now Toronto Metropolitan University, renamed in 2022 after much public outcry that the school was named after Egerton Ryerson, who played a pivotal role in developing the model for residential schools), where I was pursuing a bachelor of journalism degree. I had wanted to study at Ryerson for a few reasons. For one, it was located right in downtown Toronto, and I longed for escape from my small town. The city had long been a distant twinkle in my eye—a place where glitz and glamour and fashion excitement awaited. Now, I was finally going to be a part of that world. I still couldn't fully process that it was finally happening, even during the long drive down.

I also wanted to study at Ryerson because it had one of the best journalism programs in the country. (And, if you haven't figured it out by now, I've always wanted *the best of the best*.) I knew I wanted to write about fashion, and to work at a fashion magazine. *The Devil Wears Prada* had just come out, and TV shows like *The Hills*, *The Rachel Zoe Project*, *America's Next Top Model*, *Project Runway*, and *The City* offered an inside look at what it was like to work in the fashion industry. Journalism was my ticket into a world I so desperately wanted to be in.

Somehow, the school had accepted my application. Ryerson has a famously small journalism program—meaning it was difficult and competitive to get accepted. During my last year of high school, I spent all my extracurricular time doing reporting for the *Tribune*, our small-town newspaper, where I'd report on our high school's sports games or events. I hated doing this, of course—I wanted to write about *fashion*—but I knew I needed the writing clippings for my Ryerson application. Clearly, it paid off.

"We're so proud of you, son," Mom said about halfway through our drive.

My parents of course felt sad about the prospect of me being far away from home, but they understood that I needed to spread my wings and pursue my passion.

"You know, not a lot of kids in our community have been able to get these opportunities," she continued. "We're very fortunate you got in."

I was fortunate, I thought. Luckily, I'd had help. Our community band office had funding for undergraduate students, and thanks to my good grades in high school, I was able to have my entire tuition covered—something I still have immense gratitude for today. Without that funding, I realized that going to such a prestigious school might not have been possible. (Though I'm sure my supportive parents would have found a way.)

"Yeah, I guess I am," I said, looking out the back of the car, watching as my humble Northern Ontario roots slipped farther and farther into the distance.

After the drive—five hours that felt like an eternity—we finally arrived at the campus.

I was amazed that the whole school was located smack-dab in the middle of downtown, just off Dundas Square (basically the Toronto equivalent of Times Square). The whole feel of the city was so exciting to me—the chaotic pace, the honking, the noise everywhere. I loved it. Compared to my serene little rez life by the water, it was a total culture shock. But I loved the dirty streets and the rats and the garbage and the overstimulation, because it meant that there were a lot of people around—and when there are a lot of people around, there's a lot of opportunities around, too.

Dad pulled our car up to my residence, which was already buzzing with students and their parents, who, like mine, were helping them move in for the school year. I felt nervous—the same way you feel on the first day of school, when you have to make new friends and put yourself out there.

We checked in and then began making multiple trips up to the sixth floor and back down, to unload all my crap into my dorm room. To my surprise, I had a pretty boujee dorm room; I had no roommate, for one, and I even had my own private bathroom. Yes, my *very own* bathroom—pretty luxurious for a dorm room, no?

I met a few other students on my floor as Mom, Dad, and I continued to unpack. We tried to make things cozy—by taping my favourite posters to the wall (a *Kill Bill* poster, my favourite movie at the time), unboxing my fake desk plants, and setting up my bold-printed bedding, so the room felt a little more me.

It was all such a mad dash, and then, suddenly, my parents were saying their goodbyes.

"You be careful out here," Mom said, already beginning to cry. I was their last chicken to flee the coop, and it was particularly hard for Mom to accept that I was moving out.

"Call us after your first day," Dad said, giving me his signature awkwardly harsh hug.

This was officially my new home. I was now in a foreign city, all alone, unsupervised. The world was my oyster! The moment felt like a real turning point; I was no longer a teenager with no responsibilities but an adult in charge of my own future. An adult who had the capacity to make my own choices—good or bad. Being around a floor of new people also meant that I could be whoever I wanted to be. That I could dress however I wanted to dress. That was the best part, really. I was fucking *ready*.

I NEEDED A strong fashion look for the first day of journalism school. An outfit that said I'm studious—*cool*—not at all from a middle-of-nowhere hick town.

In Toronto, I could be anyone I wanted to be, and I wanted to be Christian Allaire, fashion journalist extraordinaire. First impressions are everything, after all. I wanted to put forward a stylish front, in the hope that it would help me to quickly make friends.

This was 2010, when business-casual style was trending, for some reason. It was the era of sleek blazers, bodycon dresses, big (*huge*) clutches, and sock buns. In retrospect, all the twenty-year-olds were running around looking like forty-five-year-old HR managers named Karen or Brian—but it was the *look*.

I rummaged through my (extremely tiny and bursting) dorm closet to see what I could conjure up. I landed on a structured black blazer, skinny black jeans, and my favourite studded Prada sneakers (sneakers I'd blown all of my money on, of course). Sure, I was nervous for my first day, but I walked into the journalism school—a small, sleek building in the middle of campus—looking right on-trend.

My morning class—Introduction to Reporting—was located in a building directly adjacent to my dorm. The commute was about three minutes, so I got to class early. I looked around at some of my fellow journalism students as we waited to be let into class.

It was a motley crew of young, eager folks. There were lots of bookworm types, some a little more fashionable than others. I had never been around so many people of different backgrounds: white, Black, Indian, Asian. A quick glance around, and I didn't see any Native kids. Based purely on aesthetics, I immediately got the sense that many of these kids wanted to be *serious* journalists—you know, the kind who travel to war-torn countries or interview politicians. I just wanted to write about clothes.

"Are those Prada?" a fellow classmate suddenly asked me, as I stood awkwardly in the hall.

"Yes," I said shyly.

She introduced herself to me as Teresa. She was bleach blond, Italian, and had a fabulous Marc Jacobs purse on, which I clocked immediately. Like me, Teresa was dressed all in black, and, to my delight, she also wanted to write about fashion.

"Yeah, one day I want to write for somewhere like *Vogue* or *Elle*," she said as she reapplied her Dior lip gloss. She was so fab.

"Me too!" I said. "I've wanted to work for *Vogue* since I was little."

"Thank god I met you," Teresa said. "I thought everyone in this program would be weird political reporters or something." We laughed.

Only five minutes in, and I had already made a friend. My master plan was working!

The classroom door finally opened, and Teresa and I sat next to each other. Obvi.

I was anxious about what was to come. I had read online about how demanding and time-intensive the undergraduate journalism program was. I knew it wouldn't be an easy road. But I was excited for the challenge. Like the brochures promised, our class size was small. There were only about fifteen students in the room.

I had taken out my notepad, ready to get underway, when our professor—an acclaimed journalist, no less—threw us an immediate curveball.

"Welcome to Introduction to Reporting. You'll actually be reporting a story today," he said. My eyes widened. *What? I've never actually reported before*, I thought. My small-town newspaper barely counted.

Our assignment was simple. We had to complete a series of "streeter" interviews, where you go up to complete strangers on the street and ask them questions in order to get quotations for a story—a way to gauge public opinion on a particular issue or topic that's trending in the news. Not only would we have to do these streeters, but we'd also need to write a story around the quotes—and the assignment was due at the end of class. Meaning, we had just a few hours to do it all.

"Off you go!" he said.

We were all in a panic. I desperately wanted to tag along with Teresa—we could help each other!—but she ran off solo. At the time, I was still painfully shy; the idea of approaching a complete stranger on the streets of Toronto almost caused me to have a nervous breakdown. Not only that, but the topic was something political, and I knew *nothing* about politics. If you'd asked me to write a story about a new designer collection, I would have aced it. But politics? I was doomed. Fail me now!

"Dad?" I said, as he picked up the phone at the other end of the line.

I was standing on Yonge Street, just a few minutes away from class. And I was paralyzed with fear; I was far too nervous and introverted to go up to strangers.

"I have to get quotes for an assignment. Can you give me one?"

I recorded his voice over the speaker phone, and changed his name to something generic like Bob Smith or Paul Brown, so that nobody could ever trace his answers back to him.

It was only day one, and I was already cheating on my homework. (Sorry, Ryerson!)

I wondered if I was truly cut out for this.

EVENTUALLY, TERESA AND I became two peas in a pod.

We were in all of the same classes. Between courses, we'd often walk over to the Eaton Centre mall to do some shopping, or to complain about our workload.

Teresa was unlike anyone I had ever met. She was outspoken, and totally unapologetic. Where I was quiet and reserved, she was blunt and boisterous; we balanced each other out perfectly. Because our class sizes were so small, we quickly became known as the fashion duo in school. Everyone knew we wanted to work at a fashion magazine—even our professors—and you could certainly tell by our edgy outfits. We often showed up looking like members of the Addams Family. But in Prada.

Everyone else in our classes wanted to be *serious* journalists, and the program was certainly catered to them. During class, we'd discuss what was going on in Syria, or what shenanigans the then Toronto mayor Rob Ford was up to. I'd often only be half listening, or online shopping on my phone. I wasn't interested in all of that; I wanted to talk about writing that was centred on pop culture, fashion, and art.

There were few students in my program who I felt I could connect with in this way. In our Reporting 101 class, Teresa and I befriended a few others. There was Tina—a nice Jewish girl who wanted to produce an entertainment TV show—and Hayley—a cool Montreal girl who liked fashion, too, and always looked effortlessly cool in her grungy denim. But during that first year of school, it became apparent to me that there were few—if any—Indigenous kids in my classes. I was probably the only one. I was shocked at this, given that Toronto had one of the largest Native populations in Canada.

Or so I had read.

I was used to not having Native friends in school, of course. But I thought Ryerson would be a place where I could finally connect with some fellow Native kids. And being away from home (and not wanting to admit I was a little homesick), I realized that I needed an Indigenous ally.

A few weeks into school, I decided to reach out to the

school's Aboriginal Student Services Centre. I had read about it in one of those cheesy pamphlets they give you on orientation day. I wanted to see if they could connect me with any other students, or perhaps at least help highlight extracurricular activities where I could possibly connect with some on my own.

"Hi," I wrote in an email. "I am an Ojibwe student in the journalism program, and was wondering if I could meet someone from the centre or be given a tour of the space?"

I got a reply back almost right away, saying they would love to show me around. *That was quick*, I thought.

I was excited about the prospect of finally meeting some other city Natives, and I thought it was super cool that Ryerson even had such a service at my disposal.

I walked over to the Aboriginal Student Services Centre and was promptly greeted at the elevator by one of the program managers. The centre was on the third floor of a wing of the campus I had never gone to before. It was an older building that hadn't yet been renovated. I was starting to get major *Indian in the Cupboard* vibes. Why wasn't the centre in one of the school's sleek, fancy new buildings?

"I'm so happy you reached out," the manager said, as she took me down a long, winding maze of a hallway. "We don't get many people reaching out. We've been trying to expand the community."

Finally, we arrived at the Aboriginal Student Services Centre. It wasn't so much a centre as it was a bona fide janitor's closet. I had expected to walk in and find a few Native students hanging out in there or studying or *something*, but instead, the room was the size of a shoebox, with one or two chairs in it— and it was totally empty. The lights were off. The whole space felt cold—and, honestly, it may have even *been* cold. It was clear that nobody had been in the room for quite some time. Cue a passing tumbleweed.

"Nobody must be here today," the program manager said.

Was there ever?

Nobody from the centre ever contacted me again after that first visit.

I can't say I was shocked at the lack of cultural support from the school. Ryerson itself was named after Egerton Ryerson, whose writings influenced the horrific residential school system in Canada—the same abusive schools that my grandmother had survived. Did I *really* expect them to care about me as a Native student? I wondered if the Aboriginal Student Services Centre was just a front. A way to look good to outsiders, to tick a box on a pamphlet. Was it even *real*? It certainly wasn't helpful to me as an Indigenous student.

I never went back.

DURING MY FIRST year at Ryerson, I enjoyed learning about the craft of writing feature stories. In class, we'd read the work of some of the greatest writers of our time—Joan Didion, Hunter S. Thompson, Truman Capote, Susan Orlean—and discuss why their pieces were so well executed. I became infatuated with the way they told stories and described people. Journalists saw the world differently. They weren't so much reporting the facts, I learned, as telling a real-life story in a way that grabbed a reader and made them understand someone else's point of view in an entirely new way.

I saw journalism as an art form.

I hated school, however.

I was always a good student, even making the honour roll in high school, but sitting in class bored me to tears. I hated sitting in a lecture hall listening to one person speak for hours. I hated writing the trivial assignments that didn't get published anywhere. I hated hearing the opinions of classmates who raised their hand during every single discussion and thought they knew everything. I was eager to enter the workforce. Naively—not even a year into school—I wanted my byline out there. I felt like school was holding me back from getting real on-the-job experience.

That's why I had to come to Toronto, wasn't it?

Hungry to get out there and get *real* hands-on job experience, I started reaching out to various fashion stylists, to see if I could assist them on their magazine photo shoots. I wanted nothing more than to be on a set, to see how clothes could come to life in a photograph. At the time, I wanted to be a fashion editor—someone who styled shoots and wrote the copy for magazine editorials. I was young and ambitious, and I was willing to work for free, so it didn't take long for stylists to take me up on the offer.

One of my first styling gigs was assisting on an editorial for *Dress to Kill* magazine, a really cool, edgy, artsy Canadian fashion magazine that I routinely bought and perused. I cold-emailed one of their stylists, Claudia, and asked if I could buy her a coffee. When we met I told her that I'd love to assist her. To my pleasant surprise, she did need help with unpacking, organizing, and then returning clothes for an upcoming shoot. "What time do you need me?" I said.

I showed up right on time to set, a cool loft space in the west end. The job was true grunt work—unpacking and organizing samples, getting people coffee—but I couldn't have been more thrilled. As I unpacked threads from Canadian designers like Lucian Matis and Greta Constantine, I was full of glee. *My first fashion shoot!*

I watched a model twist and contort herself into fabulous poses wearing even more fabulous clothes, all while a famous photographer duo from Toronto snapped frames. The model sported pieces such as an austere sheer white gown and a dramatic black and emerald feathered cape. I watched in amazement as the team analyzed almost every frame, adjusting the hemline here, or changing the necklace there, to make sure they got the *perfect* shot.

Nobody so much as made eye contact with me or said my name during the entire shoot, of course. Interns are hired as invisible help. But I was in heaven nonetheless. I finally felt like part of the world I had dreamed of for so long.

When the school year ended and summer approached, I wanted to keep my on-the-job experience going. I was *desperate* to stay in Toronto. I simply couldn't go home, back to the cows and the forest—I needed to be networking, and to go on photo shoots! Any feelings of missing home were clouded by a drive to stay in the city and make a name for myself.

During classes, I started applying to just about every internship imaginable, running the gamut from television productions to an online video game magazine. I didn't care, so long as it meant I could stay in the big city and be semi fashion-adjacent.

After countless emails, I landed my first full-time summer internship: it was at a small men's fashion publication called *Argyle*, a former luxury lifestyle magazine distributed through the national newspaper the *Globe and Mail*. This would be my first official fashion position that I could put on a resumé. Problem was, this bitch was broke. I needed to find funding for me to stay in Toronto for the summer, especially because the internship was unpaid. I had to convince my parents.

"Mom, I scored a fashion internship here this summer, and I *really* want to stay for it," I said when I called my parents' house after school one day.

There was silence on the other end. They had anticipated me coming home for the summer.

"Well," she finally said, after more begging, "we're going to have to see if the band has summer funding." My parents certainly couldn't front my frivolous summer in the city.

Turns out, though, that our band office was able to secure funding, which meant I could stay in Toronto, rent my same dorm room for the summer, and complete the internship. I felt a sense of relief.

Only, Ryerson then tried to deny it.

"This type of funding isn't accepted here," a snarly by-the-books administrator told me during their office hours while eating a messy sandwich. I had made an appointment after being told my funding was rejected. "We've never allowed this funding before."

They made the argument that summer funding was somehow different from tuition funding. Had there never been other Indigenous students at Ryerson with such funding? I, again, felt a lack of support and sensitivity from the school I was studying at. It's hard enough to receive funding for Indigenous students in metropolitan cities, but it's even harder when your school then tries to deny that funding. It seemed like a vicious cycle.

After a few phone calls from my mom—an educator herself, and a *very* convincing woman—the school finally accepted the funding. They didn't make it easy, though.

As I prepared for my summer internship, I reflected on how lucky I was—to have supportive parents, a scholarship, and funding. And yet, even with all of that, it was still an uphill struggle at times. What was it like for other Native kids who didn't have these support systems?

I felt even more pressure to make my summer internship worthwhile. And as eager as I was, I had no absolutely idea what was about to come my way.

CHAPTER 5

NGII-MKAAN NDEBWEWIN
(I FOUND MY TRUTH)

"ARE YOU THERE YET?"

I slammed on the brakes. *Shit.* I was so distracted by the incoming text message that I almost ran through a red light. The car behind me honked furiously.

"Sorry!" I screamed, as I waved a hand out the window. "So sorry!"

It was already shaping up to be an extremely busy Tuesday morning. I was in the midst of driving my boss's (very expensive) Mercedes through the streets of Toronto, running various errands along the way. And I was stressing hard—because I was now *late*.

My *Argyle* summer internship in Toronto was not going quite how I had hoped. I'd been hired to be a part-time assistant to the magazine's editor-in-chief, Joseph, three days a week. I knew it wouldn't be glamorous work, of course, but what I hadn't anticipated was having to drive around town in a car that cost more than my entire net worth. Oh, and did I mention I'm a horrible driver?

What I was *really* interested in doing at *Argyle* was assisting the magazine's fashion director, Nikolai, on his glitzy editorial photo shoots. I had come across Nikolai's work on Instagram—more like stalked him—and I loved the way he styled his models. I wanted to be him one day. Instead, I was stuck doing Joseph's grunt work, which kept piling on. But I understood that any internship was a valuable one, so I stuck with it.

The light turned green, and I pushed the pedal to the metal.

Instead of assisting on a glitzy fashion shoot or writing articles for the magazine, I was now rushing to make it to Joseph's daughter's birthday party. At Joseph's request, I had just picked up her birthday present—some sort of new pink toy—and wrapped it myself in the backseat of his car. The wrapping was horrendous: I did not have a crafty hand, and I had done a rush job. My task now was to deliver this gift to his ex-wife's house: the kid's birthday party was happening in just half an hour.

"Text me when you get there," he texted again.

The pressure was mounting.

I had never driven in downtown Toronto before, and the traffic was insane. Cars wove in front of and around me furiously. It didn't help that I drove like an eighty-five-year-old grandma. And yet, here I was, a nineteen-year-old, driving a fancy car that I had absolutely no business driving. I was terrified of scratching it, side-swiping a car (or pedestrian)—or worse, totally crashing it all together. Fashion roadkill!

This is not what I'm studying journalism for, I thought to myself, as I nervously continued to weave through traffic, try-ing to make it to the other side of the city in time.

I took a deep breath. *Okay, I've driven before. Just drive slowly and steadily.*

I crawled past more honking cars and more jay-walking pedestrians, holding my breath the entire time. I turned the radio off and drove in complete silence: No distractions.

About an hour later, I finally arrived at his ex-wife's town-house, located in a ritzy neighbourhood filled with fancy homes. I was very late to the kid's party. Traffic had been brutal, and my nervous driving had set me back even more. A nice-looking family of four was just leaving as I knocked on the front door, gift in hand. Joseph's ex-wife greeted me at the door.

"I'm so sorry I'm late," I said sheepishly. "This is from Joseph."

"Thank you," she said, taking the gift and shutting the door.

I walked back to the car, where the phone was already ringing. It was Joseph. He, of course, knew I had missed the party—he had a spidey sense for such things.

"You need to be on time for things," he barked, clearly annoyed. "Just meet me back at the office."

THE *ARGYLE* OFFICE was located in Toronto's financial dis-trict, just a fifteen- or twenty-minute walk from campus. It shared a space with another small magazine, called *Women of Influence*, which profiled high-powered women doing cool, powerful, important things.

I rushed back to work, picking up Joseph's lunch along the way. I had his lunch order memorized—usually, a schnitzel sandwich with a small side soup, from a deli spot just around the corner. As I set down his sandwich on his desk, he opened one of his desk drawers to show me something. He grinned mischievously.

"Can you take care of this?"

Inside were stacks and stacks of unpaid parking tickets. Dozens and dozens of them. Joseph, I had learned, simply refused to pay for parking—despite his ability to afford it. It was like some sort of a weird power move. I was used to seeing the unpaid tickets by now. One of my recurring responsibilities was to head down to Metro Hall to dispute the violations.

"Just make excuses for them," Joseph said. "Try to fight them."

This had become a weekly occurrence, and it looked like today would be this week's lucky day of contesting. It was punishment for not delivering the birthday gift on time, I reasoned.

So, back to the luxurious Mercedes sports car I went. I raced up towards Metro Hall—this time blasting the new Marina album—as my stomach growled because I'd had to skip lunch. I made a brief stop to gas up the car along the way. (On his card, of course.)

"Hey, kid, is that your car?" a gas station attendant inquired as I attempted to figure out the gas nozzle. I didn't have a clue how to unlatch it.

"Yeah," I lied. I didn't have time for the small chat.

"Damn," he said, looking confused. "*Good for you.*"

Was it?

I continued making my way to the parking dispute screening office and parked right near Metro Hall. By this point in the summer, I was a pro at coming up with elaborate excuses on the spot. The objective, as always, was to get as many of the tickets dismissed as possible.

Here we go.

I headed up to the counter—in one of those sad, stark city offices with bad lighting—and pulled out my hefty stack of tickets. I went down to Metro Hall so often that all of the parking clerks knew me. One regular even knew me by my first name. "Back again, I see," the kind, older Black lady said with a knowing smile. She knew the situationship here: I was just a dumb student doing what my boss asked.

"Indeed, I am," I said, quietly sliding the stack of tickets in front of her.

She pulled up and examined each one, asking why I was contesting it.

"The no parking sign wasn't visible," I told her, as she eyed the first ticket.

"The parking meter was broken; I couldn't pay it," I quipped for another. "It wasn't my fault!"

My favourite excuse, however, was the classic "I *did* pay the meter! Why am I getting a ticket?" I would say this with a slight attitude. "This must be some sort of mix-up."

After an exhaustive hour, I managed to get a good half of the tickets thrown out. Looking back, I realize the attendant likely played along out of pity—which I appreciated, every time. Whichever parking tickets I couldn't dispute would be paid off using Joseph's credit card.

"Pleasure doing business with you," I said, walking out with a much lighter stack of papers.

"See you soon," she said with a knowing smile.

The task felt like such a degrading one at the time—definitely not journalism-related *at all*. But it wasn't a total loss. After that, I could argue my way out of just about anything.

THE *ARGYLE* INTERNSHIP wasn't all humbling torture.

As I worked on more and more menial tasks for Joseph that summer, I *was* awarded bigger and better opportunities to work with Nikolai.

On my favourite days, I got to help Nikolai unpack and pack samples for his various photo shoots. Through Nikolai, I learned that brands only loaned clothes for shoots for a few days; you had to promptly pack them up and return them when you were done. It made sense to me. A photo shoot was free advertising, after all.

I loved seeing what clothes or accessories Nikolai would call in. One of the very first shoots I assisted him on was a leather gloves editorial. In his office, I unpacked bags of chic leather gloves: I would often sneak a feel of the luxurious leathers on styles by Chanel, Hermès, and more. They all *felt* expensive. Nikolai had good taste.

"I called in some more gloves from Holt Renfrew," Nikolai said, as I was just beginning to organize all of them on his desk. "Could you go pick them up?"

Holt Renfrew was a ritzy department store up in Yorkville— the bougiest part of Toronto. It was one of Canada's fanciest stores, and I dreamed of being able to shop there one day. Even having an opportunity to window-shop there was welcome.

I, of course, jumped at the task. "For sure," I said, trying to conceal my excitement.

I took the subway up to Yorkville. (Joseph did not let me

drive his Mercedes for anything other than his personal errands.) The Yorkville neighbourhood had a glossy feel to it. The streets somehow seemed cleaner, the trees more manicured.

On Bloor Street, the Holt Renfrew store stood impressively, stretching the width of an entire block. Outside, I took a moment to look at the shoppers walking around. They carried big Louis Vuitton and Chanel bags, and were clearly in a different tax bracket than mine. But the energy—the glamour, the glitz—was precisely what I had longed for *for years*. And now here I was, a part of it.

I headed inside and picked up a bag of gloves from one of the department store's public relations contacts.

"We love Nikolai," she said as she handed me the big pink bag. "We let him borrow whatever he wants from here."

"Should I add some Prada shoes for me on his tab?" I deadpanned. She only half smiled.

Given how quick the hand-off had been, I decided to spend fifteen minutes perusing the store. I had some rare time to myself, and I wanted to take advantage of it.

I beelined my way to the men's section downstairs, excited to window-shop for myself. As I was gliding down the long escalator, a big "SALE!" sign immediately caught my eye.

Nudie Jeans, my favourite designer denim brand, were on sale! There was a *whole rack* of them. Light-wash, dark-wash; baggy, skinny, slim fit. I couldn't believe it. I had dreams of owning these jeans—they haunted me. Clearly, I had to have a pair.

I was extremely broke, but I justified buying them by telling myself that they were 50 percent off, and that I would use my status card to at least save some more money on the taxes.

(In Canada, status cards are issued to Indigenous folks by their respective nations. To receive one at Nipissing First Nation, you must be able to prove that you have at least 50 percent blood quantum. In Canada, status card–carrying Indigenous people don't pay HST under the terms of the Indian Act.) Plus, I had been busting my ass for Joseph for weeks now. I convinced myself that I *deserved it.*

I brought the jeans—a black, wax-coated skinny pair—to the checkout counter.

"Great choice," said a snooty-type man in a suit. "Will that be all?"

"Yes. Oh, and here's my status card," I said, handing it to him along with my debit card.

"Your *what?*" he said. He held up the status card with a look of slight disgust.

"My Native status card," I continued. "For the tax exemption."

"I've never seen this before," he said, confused. "We don't *do* tax exemption here."

The sales associate called over one of his managers. I told them again that the status card exempts the HST. "Other stores always do it no problem," I said meekly.

They disappeared to the back for a few minutes. It was always a tad humiliating having to basically fight for the right to use a status card, especially in a fancy-schmancy store like this. But I was ballin' on a budget—my pride would have to be subdued for a second.

They returned, and the manager showed the clerk how to ring up the jeans. *Had they known all along how to do it? Were they just hoping I would give up?*

"So, you're Native," the clerk said as he folded up the jeans. "You don't *look* Native."

My face flushed. I could feel my cheeks getting hot. I was immediately taken back to my childhood days, when I was constantly told by my classmates that I didn't "look" Native enough—which, in turn, often made me feel like I *wasn't* Native enough.

This transaction was supposed to feel fun, celebratory, but instead it began to feel dirty. "How am I supposed to look?" I replied defensively.

"So, you're from a reservation?" he continued, wrapping the jeans up in tissue.

"Yes, it's called Nipissing First Nation," I said.

"Does it have a casino?"

"Not every reservation has a casino," I said, even more defensively now.

"That's cool that you can use a status card for this," he continued, oblivious to my discomfort. "You must save *so* much money. Don't you all get free education, too?"

Now I was getting pissed.

Here I was shopping in an upscale luxury store, and I was still being thought of as a freeloading Indian trying to get a handout. I was buying designer jeans, for eff's sake! Yet he was making me feel like I didn't belong.

When the purchase was over, the clerk slid the status card back to me, and I got out of the store as quickly as I could. The racism was off the charts. And yet, this was only the beginning—far from the last time someone in fashion would take a dig at my culture.

I WAS BUSY with my first year of school and completing my summer internship at *Argyle*, so I didn't have much time for a personal life.

During that first year, fellow students on my dorm floor were out getting shit-faced, downing tequila shots, and having crazy sexcapades. I would often be in my dorm room doing my homework—or plotting out my next career move. I was basically kind of a loser, so obsessed with being successful that I didn't enjoy the frivolous fun that comes with being dumb and in your early twenties. Sometimes, when my floormates would knock on my door hoping to hang out, I'd just pretend I wasn't home. I wasn't interested in partying or playing beer pong. I was fixated on making a name for myself in fashion.

I also mostly avoided a bustling social life because I was still trying to figure out who I was. I wasn't "out" during college, and nor was I convinced I was even queer.

Friends I would meet in school would automatically assume I was gay, and I'd quickly get offended. "I'm straight," I'd say defensively, unsure of the words coming out of my mouth. I avoided hanging out with people because I was self-conscious about the fact that I didn't even know who I was. Determined to deflect any personal scrutiny, I threw myself into school and work instead. I was doing my best to avoid the main issue in my life: coming to terms with myself.

But as with so many good things in life, it was a fateful out-of-the-blue moment that changed everything.

One morning, as I was walking to *Argyle*, I wandered into my local Starbucks, where I had become friendly with most of the baristas. I ordered my signature drink—a venti cappuccino with light foam, which I religiously drank like water.

"Morning," I said to one of my favourite baristas, who often didn't charge me.

"Hey, are you single?" she asked as she got to making my cappuccino.

"Yes," I said hesitantly. "Why?"

I realized I had not once thought about dating throughout my first year of school. There had been no crushes, no one-night stands, no hotties that I eyed in class. If my sex life had a soundtrack during my first year at university, it would have been the call of crickets.

"I have a friend who I'd love to set you up with," she said, handing me my nine-dollar drink.

"Oh, do you," I said, totally flustered at the concept. "Who?"

She told me his name was Johan. *Only hot people have a name like Johan*, I thought to myself. Deep down, I knew I was physically attracted to men—it's something I had felt but had repressed since I was kid. But for some reason, I decided to go along with it this time. I think it was her nonchalance about it all.

I was also intrigued at the prospect of a blind date. If there's one thing that I love in this world, it's having something set up for me. I'm lazy! I asked to see his photo.

He was, indeed, hot. Like *model hot*. Johan was a staggering six foot two, had icy-blond hair, broad shoulders, great bone structure, and piercing blue eyes.

He was totally out of my league. So obviously, I said yes.

"Okay," I said, giving her my cellphone number. "Tell him to text me."

I skipped my way to work like I had just won the lottery.

In the week that followed, Johan and I texted back and

forth. I was totally giddy—despite the gruelling, hellish work-load I was currently dealing with. There really wasn't much foreplay. A few days later, we decided to meet up for a date on College Street, where all the trendy restaurants are in down-town Toronto.

To say that I was nervous for the date is an *understatement*. It was my very first date with a boy, and only my second date *ever*. (My first date had been with a girl back in high school, one of my sister's college roommates, who—for some reason—she'd set me up with. That one had been a total awkward disaster.)

The day of my first *real* date, though, I spent hours trying to decide what to wear. I was convinced that I wouldn't be cute or cool enough for this mysterious model man. But I tried, landing on a silky black button-up shirt, black skinny jeans, and combat boots.

Johan and I met up at my place before heading over to Col-lege Street. We exchanged an awkward hug as I let him in. He smelled good, and he had a nice strong hug.

"You're tall," I blurted out. "I'm used to being the tall one."

"I like your outfit," he said, eyeing me up and down. "I have to warn you: I'm not stylish at all."

"We can fix that," I said, trying to flirt. I was nervous as hell, but was managing to play it cool.

For some reason, we decided to go up to the roof to look at the amazing skyline view of downtown Toronto—a some-what clichéd but romantic moment. I had butterflies. We were about fifteen minutes in, and I was already down *hard* for him. I couldn't tell if he was into me or not. He was a model, for god's sake! What could he possibly see in little ol' me?

We headed to College Street to have some BBQ. Eating

wings on a first date is probably the unsexiest thing one can do—yet, it somehow worked, easing the tension. The date went well enough. We had cute banter; ate great food.

Johan told me about how he was modelling but only doing it to make money during school. He went to a college nearby and was studying business. He seemed smart.

"And my friend told me you work in fashion?" he asked, mid-wing.

"Yeah," I said. "I want to work at a magazine and write about fashion one day."

"Well, you've got the look down." He smiled.

I blushed.

At the end of the date, we were saying our goodbyes outside the restaurant. I got too nervous to make a move; I couldn't even muster a peck on the cheek. Johan didn't make a move either, instead giving me a warm hug. He had told me he wasn't out to some of his family, either. I think we were both testing the waters, so to speak.

We ended up going out a few more times after that. You can fill in the blanks. Eventually, though, the romance fizzled. But for the first time in a while, I felt a kind of happiness—new and unfamiliar—like a weight had been lifted off my shoulders.

Yep, I was definitely gay.

CHAPTER 6

NAKE WAA-ZHAAYAAN
(THE DIRECTION I WANT TO GO)

MY SECOND YEAR AT RYERSON flew by. I even made a few more friends.

There was Dawna from Prince Edward Island, a fellow fashion lover in my program who dreamed of being an entertainment reporter; I loved her affinity for skin-tight leather dresses, neon purses, and cheetah-print everything. There were Britney and Melissa, identical twins and fashion bloggers who I met through a mutual friend. And Rory, who I met through the journalism program. Rory was also Indigenous, and specifically, *also* Ojibwe; he became my first Native friend in the city.

My second year at school wrapped up, summer came rolling around again, and I was determined to continue my fashion career trajectory. Having worked on photo shoots, I knew I enjoyed being on set—but I decided I wanted to be writing more in this summer of 2012. I needed some actual clippings for my portfolio. To have any chance of getting a job in this competitive industry once I graduated, I needed something tangible with my own byline on it. Plus, I was getting kind of tired of fetching people's coffees.

I desperately wanted to write for *Vogue* one day. That was my ultimate end goal—my Oz, if I were Dorothy. But seeing that I was not "American," and nor did I live in New York City, I knew I would have to very much work my way up to that.

My plan B, I decided, would be to apply for a summer internship at *Fashion Television*—the show hosted by Jeanne Beker that had basically raised me and ignited my interest in fashion in the first place. I was excited about the thought of writing some things for their website, or at least helping write the scripts for the hosts. Maybe one day *I could host*. I internally screamed at the thought of maybe *meeting* Jeanne Beker, or even working for her. That's one coffee I'd gladly fetch any day.

That dream came to a screeching halt one day, however, when I read the news: *Fashion Television* was being cancelled. It was going off the air after twenty-seven years.

Great. Where the hell was I going to work now?

Then I saw the posting online—like a fashion mirage.

Flare magazine, Canada's *top* fashion magazine at the time, was looking for summer interns in various departments. Knowing I wanted to write, I applied directly to one of their entertainment editors, Brian, who was looking for an intern to help write culture stories for the website around film, art, music, and celebrities.

I wrote a (way-too-long) cover letter explaining why I was the right applicant, and it scored me an interview. I got the news shortly after: *I was hired*. I would be an entertainment intern for Flare.com for the whole summer. It was, once again, unpaid, of course. But you might as well have told me I'd just won the jackpot.

Because now, I'd be working at a *real* fashion magazine. With actual bylines!

THE *FLARE* OFFICE was in my favourite part of town in Toronto—just off Bloor Street near Yorkville, the chi-chi part of town. The whole idea felt fancy, that I was heading into a magazine office near where the rich, chic people shopped. The magazine headquarters were housed inside the Rogers Communications building, and the sleek skyscraper was home to many of the company's other magazines as well. But *Flare* was like the favourite child—the glitziest and most impressive publication of the bunch.

At least, in my eyes it was.

I had watched *The Devil Wears Prada* almost religiously since it came out, so before even stepping into the building, I was convinced that the *Flare* office would be just like the fictional *Runway* office in the movie. I imagined the headquarters would be filled with elegant black-and-white offices, with racks of fabulous designer clothes littering the hallways. I envisioned impeccably dressed fashionistas walking into work wearing Christian Louboutin's red-bottom heels and sleek little Lady Dior bags. I wondered what the office cafeteria was like—and if fashion people actually *dared* to be seen eating at it. Compared to my *Argyle* internship, the magnitude of this job felt bigger. More thrilling. More high-stakes.

I was excited for my first day as *Flare*'s new entertainment intern. As usual, I stressed over my outfit. That morning, I rummaged through my closet, creating a mountain of disregarded clothing on my bed. "I have nothing to wear!!" I screamed to no one in particular.

After a few different try-ons—the black suit too boring; the McQueen skull scarf too try-hard—I landed on an ensemble that veered more trendy than professional. I figured, hey, if I'm going to work in fashion, I might as well have a bold fit and be noticed. This is fashion, after all: image is everything!

I decided on a navy, button-up Opening Ceremony shirt that had "NEW YORK" splashed across the front (I had indeed bought it in New York), and I paired it with my favourite Paul Smith trousers, which had golden shark teeth printed all over them. Subtle.

I arrived to *Flare* thirty minutes early, after overestimating how long it would take me to commute to the office. *Better early than late*, I thought. Before heading inside, I looked up at the tall—and somewhat intimidating—skyscraper, and I took a moment to take it in. Here I was, a kid from the rez, from the middle of nowhere, who had somehow scammed his way into working at a glamorous fashion magazine. I felt a flash of imposter syndrome; I wondered if I truly deserved to be here. I wondered if I'd fit in.

I certainly felt like I knew a lot about fashion, but this was the *big leagues*. It felt like the first day of school, when you're hoping that all of your classmates will think you're cool. Only I wasn't walking into a classroom; I was walking into an office full of fashion editors who I admired and looked up to. I didn't have any big aspirations: I just wanted them to like me.

I walked into the building and checked in with the security desk. "Hi, I'm here for my first day at *Flare*," I said nervously to the security guard, while holding a business-ready leather briefcase that had nothing inside of it. "You'll need a guest badge," he said, typing in my information.

I looked around while I waited for him to process the badge. The morning crowd coming into work wasn't at all like the one I saw in *The Devil Wears Prada*: they weren't wearing fur Prada coats, or sky-high Louboutin heels, or sleek leather Marc Jacobs purses. I was expecting a runway of statement looks, but these workers all looked so corporate, so *bland*— like they worked in banking or human resources or something. I looked down at my gold-shark-tooth pants and felt insanely overdressed. I prayed that the *Flare* floor would be a little more stylish.

"Here you go," said Mr. Security Man. "Head on up to the eighth floor."

As I walked to the elevators, I could feel his eyes on the back of my head, giving my (somewhat ridiculous) outfit the up-and-down.

I took the elevator up and met my boss for the summer, Brian—*Flare*'s entertainment editor—in the lobby area. "Good morning!" I said, way too enthusiastically.

"Welcome," he said. "I'll give you a tour."

The *Flare* office was surprisingly large. The magazine took up almost half of the entire floor. Rows and rows of cubicles lined a wall of floor-to-ceiling windows, so the office felt bright and upbeat. We walked past the fashion department, where editors were researching stories and reviewing mood boards for upcoming shoots; we walked past the copy-research department, where the fact-checkers pored over every word, comma, and apostrophe in the feature articles; we walked past the fashion closet, where all the fabulous designer clothes were kept. In the small closet, I noticed a few interns packing clothes up with frazzled looks on their faces. As someone who had assisted stylists, I understood their pain.

We then turned a corner and got to what Brian called "The Wall." On a long hallway adjacent to even more cubicles, an entire black wall was covered with all of the next issue's pages—a way to easily see the layouts in a visual way, and to check which pages were finished and which were still being worked on. "This is where our editor-in-chief, Elise, will review the issue as it's coming together," Brian explained. I took a sneak peek: my eyes instantly gravitated towards the cool, edgy fashion editorials. There were couture dresses that were fresh off the runway; cool ripped jeans; edgy skyscraper stilettos. I loved it all. Their past issues had featured big stars like Lady Gaga, Taylor Swift, and Selena Gomez on the cover, so I wondered who this issue's particular cover star would be. "We never post the cover on the wall," Brian said with a smile when I asked him. "We can't risk someone leaking it."

Near "The Wall," I took notice of a cluster of offices that were much larger than the rest—cubicles *twice the size* of the regular ones. They even had doors for privacy. I knew that these offices must belong to *Flare*'s most important people. "That's where Elise sits," Brian said as I stared at them.

Elise was *Flare*'s fierce editor-in-chief. I had yet to spot her, but as I toured the rest of the office nervously, I wondered if I'd run into her. Just the thought of seeing her scared me. Not because I had heard she was cruel or devilish, like Miranda Priestly in

The Devil Wears Prada, but because she was the *big boss.* The woman who ran the show and shaped *Flare* into what it is.

She was the most important person that I needed to impress.

Brian showed me to his cubicle, which was located directly across from Elise's, so I knew I'd run into her eventually. I peeked into her office and saw that it was empty. "If you ever have any questions, feel free to come over and ask," he said. He then showed me to my desk, where I'd be sitting for the summer. It was a cubicle at the very end of the hall, near *Flare's* digital editors. At the time, *Flare's* website was still pretty new: there were only two web editors—one for running the website, and another for managing the social media pages. I was disappointed that I wasn't sitting closer to the fashion department, where I truly wanted to be. I wanted to be near the action! *Why the hell was I stuck with the tech people?* But I was nonetheless happy to have my very own cubicle. Dare I say, I even felt a tad important—like a true part of a team.

I FOUND MY groove at *Flare* after my first two weeks on the job. Every morning, five days a week, my montage would be the same: I'd throw on some sort of ridiculous outfit, grab my venti Starbucks cappuccino, and then head out—no, *run*—to work, determined to always be on time.

One of my main tasks as the entertainment intern, I learned, was to pitch stories for *Flare's* website every day. I was excited about the prospect of finally having a byline, at a *real* magazine. At Ryerson, I was forced to write about politics or sports and other boring things for school assignments. Here, I could write about celebrities and fashion and music and *fun* things.

And the best part about it was that other people could actually read it.

Every morning, I'd get to my desk and scan the news for any trending celebrity or fashion items. Then, I'd compile a list of ideas to pitch to Brian over at his desk: "Britney Spears is hosting as a judge on *The X-Factor* for $15 million," I'd pitch. Or, "Alexa Chung is Maje's new campaign star," I'd tease. Brian would pick the best pitch, and I'd have to write it up for the website by the end of the day. There was no grabbing coffee or dry cleaning, like in my previous internship; I was actually getting real, on-the-job experience related to writing. It turns out, I had a lot to learn. My few first articles got edited to death. Like, almost completely rewritten. But slowly, I got a better sense of what the *Flare* tone was, and I soon became a pro at cranking out quick web hits.

There were a handful of other interns my age at *Flare*. Though I was so busy getting my bearings those first few weeks that I'd barely had the chance to meet or chat with any of them. But I *had* noticed them from afar. There was Cleo in the fashion news department, who was pretty, blond, and had an effortless French Girl style about her (she wasn't French—she just *seemed* French, you know?). There was Lily, in the fashion market section, and Kourtney, in the copy-research section: they were some of the only people of colour in the whole office, so I noticed them on the very first day. On the other side of the office, meanwhile, was Mia, one of the head fashion closet interns. She had a severe, cutting-edge sense of style, and stomped around the office like she owned the place. She almost intimidated me more than Elise.

"Do you want to grab lunch with us?"

I turned around from my computer after filing a web story. Cleo, Lily, and Kourtney were standing next to my cubicle.

"Pardon?"

"We're going up to the cafeteria in five minutes. Do you want to come with?" repeated Cleo.

"Sure!" I said. I had yet to make any friends at my internship, and I was excited to finally get the office gossip. I threw on my waxy black denim Diesel blazer and met them by the elevators.

We headed up to the *Flare* cafeteria, which was largely unglamorous. There was a Tim Hortons station for all your caffeination needs, and then a sad little salad bar and a hot food bar. The "caf," as we called it, became the meeting spot for Cleo, Lily, Kourtney, and me to meet up every day at lunch that summer. We became fast friends. Back at Ryerson, I had a hard time connecting with the kids in my program; those who weren't ultra-competitive or taking themselves too seriously were just flat-out weird. But only five minutes into our first group lunch date, I felt like I had known these *Flare* girls for years. They seemed like my kind of people. *Fashun* people.

"So, where are you from," asked Cleo, as we bit into our salads and sandwiches.

"I'm actually from a reservation called Nipissing First Nation," I said in between bites. "It's five hours north of here. My mom is First Nations. We're Ojibwe."

"That's so cool!" Cleo said. "I don't think I've ever met someone First Nations in fashion."

It was the first time in a long time that someone hadn't just replied, "What? *You're* Native?"

I learned that Cleo was from Montreal, Lily had roots in El

Salvador, and Kourtney was born and raised in Toronto. Over lunch, we'd gossip about our boss's weird quirks, or who's outfits we loved in the office, or where we had gone over the weekend. The three of them became my first official fashion friends—the kind I had dreamed about having as a kid—and I was loving every minute of it.

They just got me.

THE FIRST MONTHS at *Flare* flew by. It didn't even feel like a job most days; it felt fun. Like a hobby. From the sidelines, I greatly admired *Flare*'s editor-in-chief Elise, who—to my delight—was a total joy to work for. Dressed to the nines in sky-high heels and chic pencil skirts, she was always glamorous, yet always made it a point to stop me in the hallway, compliment my outfit, or ask me what I was working on. To a nobody like me, this meant the world.

I was busy writing another web story at my desk one morning when I felt a presence behind me.

"Zac Efron?"

"Pardon," I said as I took off my headphones and turned around.

"Are you a fan of Zac Efron?" repeated Brian, who was standing behind me.

"Who isn't!" I replied.

"We have an offer to interview him about his new movie," Brian said. "You should do it."

I was speechless. I had been in my internship for only a few weeks, and Brian was already giving me my first celebrity interview. I had never interviewed a celebrity before. I had never *met* a celebrity before. The only celebrity we had back on the rez was a local named Rockhead, who my cousins and I made fun of whenever we'd spot them walking the streets. (Not to be a mean girl in a high-school movie, but their head was, indeed, shaped like a rock.) Being in close proximity to real-life stars was something I had always dreamed of, and now I was being offered a whole ten minutes with one of the world's biggest teenage heartthrobs. "Thank you so much for this incredible opportunity," I said, way too eagerly. "I would love to."

Zac was in town promoting his new movie, *At Any Price*. I was told by his publicist over email that I'd be meeting Zac and the director, Ramin Bahrani, in a swanky hotel room for the interview later that week. I spent the days leading up to it thinking of fun, topical questions—preparing for the event like I was about to grill a presidential candidate or something. Brian sat down with me and reviewed the interview questions the day before. "Good luck," he said as we finished. "And don't be nervous—just have fun with it."

I was doing the interview early in the morning, just before heading into the office. My palms were sweating as I walked up to the hotel lobby to check in for my time slot. I wore the exact same outfit that I had worn on my first day at *Flare*, including the "NEW YORK" shirt that I thought was just so cool. I was directed to a publicist with a clipboard by the elevators, who would escort me up to Mr. Hollywood himself. "You must be Christian from *Flare*," she said. "We're ready for you."

When I walked into the hotel room and heard Zac's distinctive voice, I immediately blacked out. Was I really just about to interview *Zac fuckin' Efron*? The room was set up in a traditional interview style: there were two chairs for Zac and the director by the window, and opposite them was a chair for me, the Important Journalist. In my state of nervousness, though, I didn't *see* the chair for me, which in my defence was semi-concealed behind the room's weirdly tall bed. So, instead, I took an awkward seat on the hotel bed—my feet dangling above the floor like a toddler. Real professional. By the time I noticed the chair for me, it was too late to move.

The interview went well enough. I asked the standard boring questions: *How did you prepare for this role? What drew you to the script? What was the dynamic between you and the director?* Zac was kind and generous, if a dash media-trained, with his answers. Afterwards, the kind publicist asked if I'd like a photo with Zac and the director. "Of course!" I said. I posted it to my Instagram the minute I left.

I started making my way to the *Flare* offices, excited to report to Brian about how the interview went. I texted Lily, Cleo, and Kourtney the photo of me and Zac while on the way in.

"OMG," wrote Lily. "*Flare* just reposted your photo on their Twitter!"

I felt like the coolest journalist in the office. I walked into the office beaming, and headed straight to Brian's desk, feeling like I'd aced the assignment.

"The Zac interview went amazingly," I said.

"That's great," he said, not turning around from his desk. "I saw you got a photo."

"I know! He was so, so nice," I said.

"In the future," he replied coldly, "we never take photos with the talent. That's super unprofessional."

Shit. I was in trouble. I was so taken aback that I didn't even think to tell Brian that it wasn't my idea—that Zac's people had, in fact, forced the photo *on me*!

"Oh, okay," I said quietly. "Sorry. It won't happen again."

To this day, it's a lesson that's remained burned in my memory: I've refrained from asking celebrities for photos ever since. And not to brag, but I've met *a lot* of them.

MY SUMMER *FLARE* internship was coming to an end, but I was having such a fun time learning about the biz that I wanted to continue working there once school started up again. While I was interning for Brian in the entertainment department, I had met a few of the other editors on staff, and I decided I wanted to try my luck working in the fashion department next. It was where my heart truly was, after all.

My office friends Lily, Cleo, and Kourtney had all ended their internships to head back to school, and I continued to keep in touch with Lily—who is still one of my best friends. But I wasn't ready to leave just yet. I needed to brainstorm a way to stay at *Flare*.

Luckily, I had become infatuated with Mischa—*Flare*'s chic fashion news editor, whose mother was a famous Canadian designer.

Mischa had a blunt bob with even blunter bangs, and impossibly chic style—always teetering around in heels and cutesy little peplum dresses. I asked her if she needed a fall intern, but she already had one, and said to keep in touch. I made a mental note of this. I wrote this in my notepad: *Follow up with Mischa*.

As a plan B, I asked Cameron—one of the fashion editors

who styled shoots for the magazine—if she needed help. Cameron was the coolest. She had long red hair and, in my opinion, the best fashion sense on the whole team: she'd pair graphic Celine trousers with sky-high heels and a chunky Balenciaga sweater. She seemed exactly like one of the cool girls in *The Devil Wears Prada*—the type of girl I envisioned working with at a fashion magazine. She also had a quiet confidence about her; she barely spoke, but her work had an eccentric energy that more than made up for it.

With Brian's blessing, I asked her if I could be her part-time intern during the school year, to help with fashion credits or to assist her on set. Turns out, I was in luck: she *was* in need of a fall intern.

Flare wouldn't be getting rid of me just yet!

I was now entering my third year at Ryerson, and I started off the year extremely busy—juggling school and my new fashion internship. I'd often skip class and just head to *Flare* instead; I felt I was learning more there than I was in class, where we were being introduced to broadcast journalism, podcasting, and other forms of digital journalism. I didn't care about any of that. I wanted to learn about *fashion* journalism.

My professors, however, began to notice my absence.

After a particularly snoozy class one day, one of my instructors pulled me into their office. "I fear your internship is beginning to interfere with your course load," he said. I was shocked. I handed in all my assignments on time; my grades were good. *What was the big issue?* Wasn't the goal of school to hopefully get a job after graduation? "If you miss any more classes, it's going to begin affecting your grades," he continued. "Attendance in class needs to be a priority."

Fuck off, I said in my head. "Okay, I'll do better," I replied.

If I had a priority list at the time, school was at the very bottom of it. *Flare* came first.

Attempting to find myself came second.

I was still experimenting with my sexuality. I wasn't yet comfortable with the idea of being gay, and I certainly wasn't dating around much, though I decided to make it a much bigger priority during my third year. After my fling with Johan, I briefly retreated into an era of celibacy—but at *Flare*, I developed a new office crush.

His name was Thomas. He was a fellow intern in the fashion closet. Thomas was tall and lanky and had a cute blond buzz-cut, and his personal style came complete with lots of skinny jeans and studded jackets (this was the era of Tumblr and indie sleaze, after all).

Thomas was a smoker—not a super-hot trait, looking back—and he'd often pop downstairs for a cigarette, which I thought was just *so* cool and attractive. Whenever we interacted, I could feel my cheeks getting progressively more flushed. Trying to flirt with him was like watching a deer trying to walk on ice: a complete catastrophe.

My dates with Johan had awakened something buried inside me, but the feelings I had for Thomas were still super confusing. I was still pondering if I was gay or straight; the idea of being with a man romantically still felt forbidden, or dirty. I wasn't out yet to anyone I knew, and I certainly was not ready to talk to my friends or folks back home about it. My innocent flirting with a cute co-worker may seem PG-13, but at the time, the magnitude of it felt huge. Like I was taking a step towards being the person I knew I truly was.

There were some setbacks, though. Convinced I still might be straight, I also explored the idea of going out on dates with women. I met Vanessa at Ryerson through a friend: she was studying film, and we had begun casually hanging out together—sharing a similar passion for the arts of fashion and movies. I somehow convinced myself that maybe this was love, that this was a woman I could go out with. Over Facebook Messenger that year—because I was too cowardly to do it in person—I asked her if she'd ever want to go out on a proper date with me. Even as I typed it, it felt all wrong.

"What?" she replied, clearly taken aback.

"I really like you," I typed back. Real *romantique*.

She unfriended me and we never spoke again.

I took that as a sign.

WHILE I CONTINUED grappling with my identity crisis, I hated to admit that I was also missing home. At my *Flare* internship, I felt excited and fulfilled by my career path, but on a personal level, I felt lost and disconnected from my culture and community.

I had yet to meet any Native folks working in Toronto's fashion scene, like I had hoped I would. I realized I still deeply needed more Native friends, people I could connect with on a deeper level. Could I even find such friends in the fashion scene, though?

I decided the best way to do this would be to sneak into the Toronto Fashion Week shows and meet more people. Everyone who's anyone in fashion would be at these shows—maybe there would be some cool Native folks there, too. I emailed some of the event's publicists and told them that I was coming "on assignment" for *Flare*, hoping that I could get a ticket to the catwalks as a result. (There were never any such assignments; I was becoming a professional liar). The little white lie worked like a charm, though: I secured a press pass for the entire week. Free of charge. Cha-ching!

The fashion shows were held in giant makeshift tents at David Pecaut Square, just outside of Toronto's Roy Thomson Hall. After my work days at *Flare*, or in between my classes, I would promptly head down there—every day for a week straight—hoping to network and see what the latest fashion trends were. In the process, I scored some nosebleed seats to the shows of some of the biggest Canadian labels of the moment, including Greta Constantine, Linda Lundström, and Mackage. I didn't care that I wasn't in the front row: in the nosebleeds, I squinted to see the models with total glee.

I ended up meeting my first Native fashion friend at the Linda Lundström show. Her name was Cara, and I spotted her sitting a few rows up from me. I noticed her because she was wearing this giant fur coat and these fabulous beading earrings that caught the light just right. The look basically screamed, *I'm Indigenous, and I love fashion too!* I simply had to meet her.

"I love all of your jewellery," I said to her as we and other guests started filing out of the tent post-show.

"Thank you!" she replied. "I actually made all of it."

I learned that Cara was an Indigenous jewellery designer in Toronto. And she was even Ojibwe—just like me! We chatted about the reservations we came from, and how long we'd lived in Toronto (most of her life, I learned). One Facebook friend request and then, a few days later, Cara came over to my apartment to show me some more of her jewellery pieces, which I wanted to photograph and write about for my personal fashion blog. (Yes, I had one—but nobody except my friends read it.)

Unpacking her pieces onto my kitchen table, Cara began to tell me more about the inspiration behind some of the striking jewellery, which she made by hand in her home studio. "This pendant is actually inspired by the Ojibwe medicine wheel teachings," she explained, pointing to a diamond necklace that was shaped into a circle divided in four, with different colours in each quadrant.

I was very familiar with the medicine wheel teachings: my mother and grandmother had taught them to me. In Ojibwe culture, the medicine wheel represents living a balanced life. The four colours represent the four directions and elements, and the wheel is meant to symbolize the importance of living with a spiritual, physical, mental, and emotional balance. Holding up Cara's necklace, I realized that my spiritual, mental, and emotional well-being were currently totally out of whack. I missed home.

Admiring the rest of her pieces—which included a set of four sterling silver rings that spelled out "N8IV"—I realized it was the first time I had seen our Indigenous culture modernized in such a chic, fashionable way. "Your pieces are so beautiful," I told her. "Your stuff should be in *Flare* magazine! I intern there, and I can totally show these photos to some of the editors."

"That would be amazing!" she replied. "I've tried to email and pitch a few of the magazines here, but nobody has ever been interested. They never reply to me."

A lack of Native representation in the fashion industry was nothing new to me; I had never seen Indigenous style in magazines growing up. But at that moment, I *was* shocked that someone as fabulous and talented as Cara had yet to be noticed by anyone in the Toronto fashion scene, especially because it was so tiny. It was almost as though they'd have to be deliberately *trying* to ignore her work. Then and there, something clicked in me: I suddenly understood the bigger value my position in fashion could bring to the industry as a whole. *If nobody else was going to write about Native fashion*, I thought to myself, *then I'd simply have to do it myself.*

I pitched a short profile of Cara's work to one of *Flare*'s web editors and never got a reply. This was going to take some work.

MY FALL FASHION internship was nearing its end, and I was having a blast assisting Cameron on set for her different shoots. Cameron ran a tight set—she was a clean freak and extremely particular, and would have me do things like tape the bottom of shoes so that they didn't get scratched while the models wore them. I was helping her pack up some clothes for an upcoming editorial when she shared some news with me: the magazine was getting a new editor-in-chief.

Rumours quickly swirled around the office about whether Elise was leaving on her own accord, getting pushed out, or, worse, if she was getting dramatically fired. As a lowly intern, I was not privy to any of the details—but I *was* obsessed with getting to know just who this new boss would be.

Her name, I learned, was Melinda. Her name sounded just like the fictional *Devil Wears Prada* editor. All I knew about Melinda was that she had previously been an editor at *Elle* in New York City, so she instantly possessed a prestigious fashion cachet. Nobody in Toronto knew anything about her, and in Toronto's small circles, *everyone* knew everyone.

I was never formally introduced to Melinda, but I began spotting her around the office. She had a bookish quality to her. Where Elise was always in stilettos and fabulous dresses, Melinda looked more, let's say, *studious*. On my first sighting, she was wearing clunky, pragmatic shoes—*flats*—with a long pleated skirt and a wool cardigan. The snarky comments from editors and interns instantly came flooding in. "*Did you see what Melinda is wearing?*" Mia snickered to me on Melinda's first day, with a not-so-subtle tinge of disgust. Melinda did not strike anyone as a fashion girl, let alone a fashion girl running a national fashion magazine.

And it soon became apparent that she wasn't quite the right fit.

Later that week, I was helping Cameron organize sunglasses for an accessories story. In the fashion closet, we had virtually every style of sunglasses you could think of. There were big, bug-eyed shades; sleek cat-eyed sunglasses; and tiny nineties shades. "I'm gonna pick out the best ones to show Melinda," Cameron said, carefully perusing the assortment.

Cameron had not said much about our new editor, but based on how many times we would have to call in new items—or rethink whole photo shoots entirely—she didn't have to say anything. Melinda was clearly not easy to work for.

I returned to my cubicle after organizing the rest of the sunglasses. My desk wasn't far from the fashion closet, so I could hear Melinda when she arrived to meet with Cameron for the run-through. My eavesdropping mode instantly activated, and I rolled my chair a few inches closer to listen.

"These are some of the biggest styles and trends of the season," Cameron said in her calm, elegant manner. "And I think we have a great mix of brands and advertisers, too."

"I feel like we can make this assortment . . . smarter," Melinda said. "Is there a way we can tie in some of the new books coming out this season?"

One of Melinda's biggest missions for *Flare*, I learned, was making the magazine more intellectual. And now here she was, trying to turn a cute sunglasses story into a think piece about books. The message was confusing.

"Books?" Cameron said. She was far too shy and diplomatic to say it, but I knew exactly what she was thinking. *This is stupid.*

"What if we pair each pair of sunglasses with a book," Melinda continued. "Maybe it's sunglasses inspired by some famous book characters." It wasn't a totally bad idea—though it was completely out of left field, and Cameron was left with virtually no time to execute the new vision for the project.

When Cameron got back to her desk, I heard her let out a long quiet but dramatic sigh.

Melinda's anti-fashion editorials continued. During a run-through about looks for a cover shoot, I overheard her telling Cameron that all of the pieces were *too* fashion. "Can we call in some leggings," she suggested. "I think we need to dress this down." Cameron sighed again. Suddenly, my dream fashion internship seemed to be turning into a nightmare. You could feel the tension around the entire office, especially from the fashion and art departments, which were often made to work late while dealing with Melinda's demands.

By the time my fall fashion internship was over, and it was

time to break for the holidays, more than half of the *Flare* staff had quit or moved on to another publication. It was my first taste of how cut-throat the industry can be. Many of the staff simply couldn't handle Melinda's specific new vibe for the magazine. But truthfully, I secretly admired her unrelenting vision. At least she had a point of view.

On the last day of my fall internship, Melinda even came to our "goodbye interns" lunch in one of the conference rooms and gifted us with a swag bag of free beauty products.

"I think it's super cool that you're First Nations," she said, after asking me where I was from. I told her that I was Ojibwe. "We need more Indigenous people in fashion."

Melinda herself exited the magazine just a few weeks later, in January. And a few years after that, *Flare* shuttered its print magazine entirely.

Fashion, I learned, was fickle. One day you're hot—the next, you're not.

But one thing was clear: fashion *did* need way more Indigenous people.

CHAPTER 7

GCHI-NDAMTAAWIN
(A GRINDING, BUSY TIME)

BY THE END OF MY third year at Ryerson, I had only one thing on my brain: New York City.

New York City was where I wanted to live. Where I wanted to work. Where I wanted *to exist*.

It's one of the world's fashion capitals, after all. Where else would I be?

Toronto was certainly a fun city to go to school in: it broke me out of my small-town shell and introduced me to all sorts of people—including (finally!) Indigenous people who loved fashion just as much as me. My time in Toronto was invaluable for this reason. However, I grew bored of the city rather quickly. Sure, I had idolized "the big city" as a kid, but by year three of school, Toronto had lost its sparkle.

For one, every fashion event or party had the same people at it. The fashion scene felt small, so much so that it even felt like a small town at times—the exact thing I was trying to escape. I had also visited just about every cool store or boutique across the city, and gone to every landmark and tourist attraction.

I was, dare I say it, bored. Bored of the city I'd once glamorized in my head.

New York City, however, felt like a whole new world to explore. A world with even bigger prizes, bigger opportunities, and, yes, higher stakes. I felt the sense of excitement for New York that I had once felt for Toronto. I dreamed of working at a big fashion magazine like *Vogue*, and if I wanted to be a serious fashion journalist, I decided there was simply nowhere else I could be; I needed to go right to the heart of the fashion world.

Only problem was, I had absolutely no idea how to get to the Big Apple. I don't mean logistically, of course, because I would have hitchhiked there if need be—my bags packed only with ambition and drive. No, I mean I had no idea how I would get there *legally*. I was a Canadian citizen without a U.S. green card, and nor did I have dual citizenship. A quick Google search taught me that I couldn't just move to the United States once I graduated, no matter how much I wanted to. As an Indigenous person whose Ojibwe tribe has roots both in Canada and the United States, I felt this barrier was illogical. And unfair.

Then again, when are Indigenous people ever treated fairly?

One Sunday night during the school year, I called my parents back home. It was a ritual I did every weekend to keep in touch, and to see what drama or happenings were going on back at the rez. After my mom filled me in on which of my aunties were squabbling—given she has seventeen siblings, there's always *some* sort of fight going on!—we got to talking about my schoolwork.

"Random question," I asked, "but what do you think it would take for me to intern in New York this summer?"

"That sounds expensive," she said bluntly, unfazed by my lofty ambition. "But with your status card, I believe you're allowed to work in the States."

My status card! Why hadn't I thought of that? That shiny piece of plastic that had caused such confusion in Holt Renfrew while buying my overpriced jeans meant that I *could* actually legally live and work in the United States, without being a citizen.

Turns out, I'm protected under the Jay Treaty—a 1794 agreement between Great Britain and the United States that states that both First Nations and Native Americans—meaning, Indigenous people in both Canada and the United States today—are able to travel freely across the border. Of course, Indigenous people know that borders are a colonial construct. Prior to colonization, there were no passports or green cards or status cards required; the land was ours to explore as we wished. I was surprised to learn that there was still a hint of this spirit alive: the United States was now mine to explore, just as I'd always hoped and dreamed. My status card would be my golden ticket—my ticket to New York City, and to my dreams coming true!

Now, I just needed to find a job.

DURING THE SPRING semester of my third year, I began plotting my next steps. I started by researching New York internships. Sure, my internships at *Argyle* and *Flare* already looked impressive on my resumé—I was ahead of the game, so to speak—but if I wanted a big New York City job after I graduated, I realized that I would need New York fashion experience first.

One day, during the middle of the school week, I looked up summer internships on my laptop in Ryerson's library space, where I often went to do work. The library building had those bad fluorescent lights that instantly give you a migraine, but for some reason, I always liked it there, even if it smelled like dust. It was one of the few spaces where I could actually focus. In some places in the building, the cell reception was super dodgy, which meant I couldn't distract myself on my phone. Bypassing the floors of musty-smelling books and small study rooms, I'd always nab a spot on a quieter upper floor, where there were fewer people and distractions around.

As I browsed the internship options, I saw, to my surprise, that all the major fashion magazines were already posting their summer internships on listing websites such as *Fashionista* or *Intern Queen* (both of which I checked religiously, of course). *Shit, am I too late?* In a panic, I began applying to them all: I fired off my resumé to all the major publications: *Elle*, *Vogue*, *Harper's Bazaar*, *W*, *Glamour*, *Teen Vogue*, *InStyle*. No magazine was off limits: if they were based in New York and related to fashion, I applied.

A week went by and I checked my email religiously, while only half listening during my classes. I hadn't heard back from a single application. Was I not good enough? *I've been interning for two damn years!* But instead of feeling defeated, I went back to the drawing board and cast a wider net. Back at that dungeon of a library the following week—in the exact same study room where you could hear a pin drop—I began looking through the internships at smaller, more obscure New York magazines. I combed through all the fashion internship listings, looking for one that sounded even *remotely* interesting or up my alley. I was beginning to panic slightly.

That's when I saw the listing for *Interview*.

I had been collecting *Interview* magazines since I was a kid. It was originally launched by the iconic pop artist Andy Warhol, but later purchased by Brant Publications. I loved how big and bold the magazine was—like a coffee table book. Since *Interview* was an artsier, more indie magazine than the major ones like *Vogue* or *Elle*, their shoots were way more experimental and wild. As a fashion-loving kid, *Interview* had fulfilled my appetite for the avant-garde, yet they always managed to have A-list stars on their covers, too. It was the cool magazine *everyone* wanted to be in.

To me, it seemed like the perfect magazine to work for.

As luck would have it, *Interview* was looking for summer interns to work in its fashion closet. The job listing was simple enough: "Must be able to assist on photo shoots, and help with packing and unpacking samples." I had done this aplenty at *Flare* and *Argyle*, so I felt confident that I was qualified. I looked up the magazine's masthead and quickly cold-emailed their fashion assistant, a woman named Jessica. I sent her my resumé and a thoughtful but concise note about how I was a long-time *Interview* fan and why I would be a great fit for the internship. I didn't expect much of a reply, but to my surprise, she replied just an hour later.

"Thanks for your application, Christian," Jessica wrote. "Are you available to come in for an interview?"

I couldn't believe it. I almost screamed with joy in the library (but remembered it was a "quiet floor.") *"Yay,"* I whispered. We secured a date and time for the interview, a week from then. The fact that I wasn't actually based in New York City didn't faze me: I booked a flight to New York immediately, on the Visa card my parents had gotten me for emergencies only. This was a *fashion* emergency!

The thought of telling Jessica that I wasn't actually based in New York City didn't seem like an option at the time. The fact that I had simply gotten a reply—*some sort of reply*—was something I couldn't risk jeopardizing. I was buzzing with excitement and immediately called my parents outside the library building.

"So, I have an early birthday present request," I said to my mom, bypassing a hello. This was in March; my birthday was months away, in June.

"Oh, do you," she replied, unfazed, as usual, by my neurotic call.

"I have an internship opportunity in New York, and they want me to interview in person next week," I said. "Can I go? *Please.*"

I was met with silence, and continued to make my case.

"I'll find a super-cheap hotel, and I'll only be there for the weekend. I won't miss school. This is a once-in-a-lifetime opportunity!"

There was another beat of silence. "Only because it's for your future," my mom said after deliberating. "But you be *careful* down there."

Bye-bye, boring Toronto—I was officially heading to the Big Apple!

I **LANDED IN** New York City the day before my internship interview.

I had been to New York City on vacation a few times growing up, so the island of Manhattan wasn't completely foreign to me. But this was my first time embarking on a solo trip, and it was certainly the first time I was up for a big dream job.

The *Interview* office, I learned, was downtown in New York's trendy SoHo neighbourhood, which is lined with designer shops, trendy restaurants, and old time-y cobblestone streets. Compared to the major magazines—which are all located in corporate midtown offices—*Interview* had a cooler, more underground feel. An edge, if you will.

I booked a weekend stay at the New Yorker hotel in midtown, on the west side. It was an old art deco–style hotel with surprisingly affordable rates. My room, which barely fit a double bed and my suitcase, might as well have been a presidential suite at the Plaza: I felt *glamorous* in it. Instead of going out and exploring the city like a normal young student would on their first night in New York, I stayed in and prepped for my interview— determined to land it at all costs. I couldn't afford not to.

The next morning, I (obviously) tortured myself over what to wear, though my luggage was spilling over with an abundance of options. *This is New York*, I convinced myself after several outfit try-ons; *everyone wears black*. I landed on a black blazer, a black tee, and black leather pants—an outfit combo that, I felt, made me look sleek and cool, yet still professional. I also wore my favourite studded Diesel sneakers. I admit, I looked cool.

I took the A train downtown, leaving extra early because I had no idea how to navigate the New York subways. Along the way, I was almost kicked in the face by one of those buskers who twirl and flip around the subway poles for money. Emerging in SoHo, I walked past the shiny Dior and Chanel stores before I finally got to the *Interview* building a few minutes early. *Breathe,* I said to myself before entering. *You got this. Be cool.*

I was told by the lobby's one security guard—an older man who looked like he'd worked there *for ages*—that *Interview* was located on the second floor. "Head on up," he said, barely looking at me. I rode the elevator up, my heart racing. To say that I was nervous would be an understatement. The elevator doors whipped open, and my eyes were immediately met with a gigantic Andy Warhol painting of Mao Zedong, the infamous chairman of the Chinese Communist Party. Because of *Interview*'s ties to Warhol, it suddenly dawned on me: *Holy shit, is that a real Warhol painting?*

Before I could inspect it closer, though, the secretary at the desk in front of the painting greeted me with a quick hello. "How can I help you?"

"Oh, hi, I'm here for an interview with Jessica," I said nervously. "For the summer fashion internship. My name is Christian."

"Okay, let me call her," she said, picking up the phone. "You can wait in the kitchen area."

The kitchen area was a tiny little space just down the hall from reception—a room big enough to fit a sink, a fridge, and a little bistro table. I had only seen a hint of the office, but it all looked like someone's apartment—not like a fashion magazine office at all. The hardwood floors were old and creaked with every step. I thought about how this job interview stood in between me and my New York future. I could feel my heart beating out of my chest.

"Are you Christiannnnn?" I heard a Valley girl–style voice exclaim behind me as I sat in the kitchen.

Jessica, the fashion assistant, walked into the tiny space with Carla, who was introduced to me as the magazine's assistant market editor. Both were dressed head to toe in black and stilettos. I felt an instant sense of relief that I, too, had dressed like a vampiric goth. *Phew!*

"Yes! So nice to meet you," I said as I stretched out my hand professionally.

"Hi," said Carla coldly, not extending her hand back. She looked my outfit up, down, and up again. "Have a seat. Do you want a water or anything?"

I sat at the bistro table while Carla went to get me a glass from the kitchen cabinets. "Oh wait, we don't have any clean glasses," she deadpanned. "Can you drink out of this tiny bowl?" She placed a bowl full of water on the table. I awkwardly took a sip from the bowl, like a dog. They began asking me the standard questions. Where had I interned so far? Why did I want to work at *Interview*? Who were my favourite designers?

"And wait, you're based in Canada?" asked Jessica, looking over my resumé.

"Yes, but I have dual citizenship," I lied. Explaining the complexities of being Native, and how the Jay Treaty works, seemed like a waste of time. All they needed to know was that I could work here legally. "I'm based in Toronto, but I was planning on being here in New York for the summer anyway," I lied again.

The lies flowed out of me with ease at this point.

"Okay—well, we think you'd work," said Carla. "So, when can you start?"

I squealed internally. *Can it really be this easy?!* I tried to play it nonchalant. "Amazing. I'm done with my semester in May, so any time after that," I said.

"How's June 1?"

"Great!"

I didn't even ponder the fact that I would need time to find a place to live for the summer. Or how I would afford to spend a summer in Manhattan, one of the most expensive cities in the world. All of those details seemed like a non-issues. Later problems.

BACK IN TORONTO, I finished off my third year and began packing for my big, exciting summer in New York. My friend Teresa—who also aspired to work at a fashion magazine one day—came over to help me choose some outfits for the internship.

"You'll obviously need a lot of black," she said, handing me my favourite black skinny Nudie jeans. Teresa, a fellow all-black wearer, pulled more pieces from my closet and handed them to me to stuff in a suitcase. "I can't believe you got an internship in New York. I feel like you're going to get hired there and never come back."

"And leave you stranded here at Ryerson all alone?" I teased. "Maybe."

I was nervous about making new friends in the big city for the summer. In Toronto, Teresa was my one best friend, and I wished I could just take her with me. I thought about how hard it had been to make connections here in Toronto, and I wondered if it would be any easier in the Big Apple. Were there even any Indigenous people in fashion in New York? *There has to be*, I thought—it has four times the population of Toronto! Still, the concept of having to make connections all over again felt slightly scary.

We cracked open a bottle of cheap wine as we got to laying out all the rest of my prospective ensembles. I packed a heavy rotation of black shorts and dress pants, and then all my fun shirts, including a grey-and-black camouflage-print Marc Jacobs button-up that I wore constantly.

"What's this," Teresa asked, pulling a beaded medallion necklace from my closet.

"Oh," I said sheepishly, "my aunt made me that." I placed it back on the necklace stand.

"It's sick! You should bring it," Teresa said.

"Maybe," I replied. I hadn't considered bringing any of my Indigenous pieces. To me, they all felt so traditional—not very hip and current, or fit for the Big Apple. I thought about the way that Carla, the *Interview* editor, had given my outfit a hard deliberation during my job interview; I needed to play it safe and to bring my fashion A game. Traumatized by years of being told I didn't "look Indigenous" enough, I wondered if they'd think I was weird for wearing such cultural pieces; it felt embarrassing to wear that stuff. I needed to wear my *cutting-edge* designers.

I didn't pack the medallion necklace.

I LANDED IN New York City just a few days before June 1. I had a week to get settled before my internship started. The drive to Manhattan from the airport felt like a movie scene: the sun was shining bright, and the jaw-dropping skyline came into view as we entered the Lincoln Tunnel. It all felt so surreal.

The cab dropped me off at my home for the summer. I was staying in a tiny room in the student residences at the Fashion Institute of Technology, which rented them out for cheap during the summer while students were away. The area was less than glamorous—in an industrial part of Manhattan near the Port Authority bus station and Madison Square Garden. The room was equally no-frills: It had two single beds that were abnormally high off the ground, and two giant windows with no curtains. (The sun would blind me awake every morning.) There was a cheap wooden desk on one side of the room, and an industrial-looking bathroom on the other. The room felt cold.

I, however, was elated.

I used my first week in the city to get my bearings and explore. I took long walks in Central Park and did some shopping in SoHo, trying to familiarize myself with what was around the office; I even journeyed down to Brooklyn, which I heard had the best vintage shops (it does). My main mission was to get to know the subway system, which seemed like you needed a master's degree to comprehend. There were so many different trains and paths, all of which had different letters, numbers, and colours on them. I got lost more than once. But eventually, I got the hang of it.

The first day of my *Interview* internship came rather quickly. That morning, I put on my best all-black outfit—my go-to *Interview* uniform all summer long—and headed downtown on the A train. I got to the office building and rode the elevator up to the second floor, where I checked in with the same secretary who had greeted me for my job interview. Again, I took notice of the gigantic Warhol painting.

"Hi! I'm here for my first day," I said.

"Cool. Jessica is in the fashion closet down the hall. You can go in," she said.

I walked down a long hallway towards the fashion closet. I had only seen the kitchen during my interview, so I was excited to see what the rest of the office looked like. And, more importantly, what the fashion closet looked like.

The old hardwood floors creaked loudly as I approached—you could hear people coming from a mile away walking down that hallway. To the right of the hall was a set of glass doors, and inside, I could see racks and racks of clothing. *This must be the fashion closet.* Farther down the hall was another set of glass doors, which I later learned was where the rest of the editorial staff was located.

I entered the fashion closet and saw three or four interns packing up clothes inside garment bags. Rap music was playing loudly. To the left was Jessica, who was sitting by her giant Mac computer at her desk. "Oh, hi, Christiannnn," she said in her slightly Valley girl tone. "Welcome."

"Thanks!" I said as I put my bag down.

"Everyone, this is Christian, he's one of our new interns this summer," Jessica proclaimed loudly. The other interns said a quick hello and immediately got back to packing. They all had a frantic look on their face.

"So, we're doing all our shoots for the September issue right now," Jessica continued, as she typed furiously on her computer. "It's a little bit of a crazy time here. Could you go to the conference room down the hall and help pack up some of those samples?"

"Sure," I said, excited to get to work.

I walked down the long hallway towards a smaller conference room on the left, which was entirely lined with more racks. I had never seen so many fashion samples in an office before; there were hundreds and hundreds of clothes. I peaked at some of the labels. All of the big luxury brands were there: Dior, Prada, Chanel, Louis Vuitton, Gucci.

Heaven!

I instantly zeroed in on the Chanel pieces in particular. The fashion house had just shown a pre-fall collection in Dallas that featured many Native American–inspired pieces, including Navajo-style ponchos and big feathered headdresses. It was a total ripoff of my cultural regalia—not to mention a cliché.

In the small conference room were two more interns packing up clothes.

"Hi, I'm Christian, I'm new," I said timidly as I walked in.

They introduced themselves as Damian and Shelley, both of whom had started their internships a month before me, I learned.

"This is kind of crazy," I continued, looking around at all of the clothes. "Are there always this many samples in here?"

"To be honest, yeah," said Damian. "It's always chaos here."

I spent the rest of the day—*all day*—packing up the clothes in garment bags. There was a rigorous system we had to follow, which involved taking photos of every single garment that was packed up, using a single digital camera that all of us interns had to fight for. Then, you zipped up the bag, put a label and return address on it, and brought it to our dedicated returns rack, where another lucky intern would be responsible for returning it (or a fashion brand would send someone to come pick it up). Once that was done, you'd move on to the next brand— scouring the racks for all the pieces by that brand, and do it all over again. It was endless. It was like a military operation—a fashion boot camp.

I was dripping in sweat by the end of my first day. I realized that my fashion internships at *Argyle* and *Flare* had essentially been child's play: this was the *big leagues*, baby.

SINCE I HAD travelled all the way to New York for this intern- ship, I decided to come in five days a week. If I was only going to be there for three months, I wanted to make as much of an impression as I could within that short amount of time. Yes, this was full-time unpaid labour, which is *definitely* illegal now- adays, but I didn't see it like that at the time. I saw it as a rare opportunity to infiltrate New York's fashion world, and it felt like it was a true privilege to do so. (Thanks to the financial support of my parents and Nipissing First Nation's summer student funding, of course.)

After my first week, I started to get a feel for what the rest of my summer would look like. If we weren't packing up clothes for a shoot, we were picking up or dropping off clothes for another shoot. On the Monday morning of my second week, I came in at 10 a.m. sharp and headed straight to the fashion closet, won- dering what awaited me today. Jessica would always already be in the closet, checking her emails or tidying up the closet from the night before. All of the editors worked around the clock.

"Hi, Christian," she said. I'd barely stepped a foot into the closet. "Can you go pick up two garment bags at Prada?"

She handed me a yellow Post-it note with the address on it and a MetroCard to get there. Off I went on the first pickup of the day. (Sometimes, there would be as many as three or four pickups across Manhattan.) The *Interview* interns were basically glorified messengers: *Interview* had little to no budget for anything and got by on free labour, so the interns would do all the sample trafficking for all of the photo shoots.

On my way to Prada, I rode the subway all the way uptown, then had to walk three long avenues to get to the brand's offices, which were located at the most western tip of the island. It was my first time seeing a big designer headquarters in person. The Prada offices were marked by a discreet door that had a subtle "Prada" logo on the buzzer.

"Hi, I'm here to pick up for *Interview*," I told the receptionist after being buzzed in.

"It'll be right out," she said coldly in the minimal space, never once looking up from her laptop.

A Prada intern soon greeted me at reception with two hefty messenger bags, both filled with weighty wool and fur coats. *Interview* was doing an outerwear editorial, and the combined weight of the two garment bags made it feel like I was carrying a dead body—possibly two.

"Are you going to be able to carry these?" the intern asked with a slight tinge of pity on her face.

"I'll manage," I said with a laugh, already sweating as I hobbled out the door.

Sure, it was a degrading task, but on the plus side, carting around heavy garment bags all summer—in extremely hot and humid temperatures, no less—got me into the best shape of my life. What I wasn't gaining in muscle mass, I was shedding in water weight, due to excessive sweating. I didn't mind the heavy lifting—I was getting *ripped*! Plus, in the process, I was getting a rapid-fire tour of Manhattan and all of its luxury designer showrooms—making pit stops at Valentino, then Dior, then Versace, then Chanel. Sometimes, I'd run into fellow fashion interns along the routes—they, too, lugging overweight bags.

When I got back to the office from Prada, I plopped down the samples and took photos of everything. It was during these brief minutes back at the office that the interns would take a moment to chit-chat. There was a steady crew of us—about ten interns. There were two head interns who had been there the longest: Jasmine was a pretty Filipino girl who dressed in edgy, all-black outfits, and she had an intimidating air about her; Matteo, meanwhile, was a flamboyant Italian gay who wore the loudest and most colourful outfits I'd ever seen. If I had a question about how to do something, I would ask either of them how to do it. Then, there were the newer summer interns like me, Damian, and Shelley, all of us obsessed with the world of style.

Later that afternoon, Carla came into the fashion closet, teetering in her sky-high Tom Ford stilettos. She looked for the first intern she saw, narrowing her gaze onto me. "Hi," she said. I was unsure if she even remembered my name. She looked me up and down. "I'm doing a beauty shoot tomorrow and we need a bunch of sand for the backdrop. Could you go out and find sand and text me the options," she asked. "I need it to be a specific colour and texture."

"Sure," I said enthusiastically. Off I went in search of sand. The glitz! The glamour!

My first pit stop was at a Home Depot, a store I had rarely set foot in before. I went to the garden section and found options for gravel and potting soil, but no sand. A bust. Next up, I headed to a pet shop down the street. *This is not the fashion experience I'd envisioned*, I thought to myself. I headed to the amphibian section and found a large bag of reptile sand. I texted Carla a photo and waited for her approval.

"Yes, please buy it."

The bag weighed a ton—more than any of the Louis Vuitton or Chanel garment bags I had been carrying. I could barely take ten steps without a breathing break. Even so, I didn't dare take a taxi (I was too broke!) or ask for an Uber back to the office (I was too shy!); instead, I lugged that bag of sand across SoHo, my arms burning in pain. People stared; kind strangers asked if I needed help carrying it down the street. *New Yorkers are so nice*, I thought to myself, given everyone typically calls them jaded or mean. It was back-breaking work—literally—but I did it with a smile on my face. Because for every bag of sand I carried across town, I'd get to step inside the world of high fashion. To me, it was worth the price of admission.

The next week, for instance, I was rewarded for all of my bitch work. Jessica needed an intern to assist on a couture shoot the magazine was doing, and I was the lucky guy picked to help. The magazine was shooting Karlie Kloss, then an emerging model (who is now one of the fashion industry's top models). At the time, I had no clue who she was—but somehow, I found myself travelling across Manhattan with this glamazon in a rented RV, helping the stylist dress Kloss up in elaborate creations from Jean Paul Gaultier, Dior, Valentino, and Viktor&Rolf. We shot her guerrilla-style on the streets, even making a pit stop at a grungy skate park. As I watched the angsty skater teens do kickflips alongside Kloss, who was striking her best poses in ethereal Schiaparelli and Armani looks, it all felt so cool and spontaneous.

The New York fashion scene, I was learning, was *fucking awesome*.

IT WASN'T ALL fun and games, though. The days at *Interview* were long and gruelling. Sometimes, some of the fashion industry's top stylists would come in for run-throughs, and we were instructed not to look them in the eye. On one occasion, a new intern *did* dare to look a top stylist in the eye—and was later yelled at for it. But as with any job that works you to the ground, the experience quickly created a bond between me and my fellow interns. Any fear I had of not making friends in the city rapidly disappeared when I realized I would be working twelve-hour days with the same people all summer long. I mean, what brings people together better than shared trauma?

When Jessica was away from her desk, us interns would talk about the designers, models, and celebrities that we loved. We'd talk about which bars we went to over the weekend; which parties we perhaps drank too much at. We'd hold up clothes and give our opinions on them. "I hated this collection," Jasmine would say. "*Ayyy*, no, I thought it was really pretty," Matteo would retort. The more we got comfortable with each other, the more we let our guards down and became friends; we became a twisted little fashion family of sorts.

Jasmine and Matteo, the most senior interns, kept track of all the samples that brands had forgotten to pick up from recent shoots—and sometimes, they'd even throw us more lowly interns a bone by giving us a free pair of jeans or sunglasses. There was lots of stealing that went on in that fashion closet: one time, a few unnamed interns even went home with pricey Chanel bags. I, meanwhile, was given a few pairs of Celine sunglasses that were far too large for my face. Even so, I wore them to death that summer, feeling hip and on-trend. This was the era of Phoebe Philo's Celine, after all.

After work, sometimes as late as 9 or 10 p.m., the interns would all go out for drinks, often to gossip about what had happened that day. One night, after a particularly gruelling day, we decided to head out for cocktails at Surf Bar—a kitschy, trendy bar in Brooklyn that had tropical drinks and sand on the floor. (*Sand?* Triggered!)

On our way there, Jasmine, Shelley, Matteo, me, and a new intern named Shaylene all chain-smoked American Spirit cigarettes. I didn't smoke, but I wanted to fit in with my cool New York friends, so I did that night. The *Interview* interns were cooler than any friends I'd ever had in Toronto. They partied, did drugs, dressed cool, knew about the coolest vintage stores or parties happening in the city. As a kid from the rez, I felt totally out of my league—but knowing nobody else in the city, I didn't have a choice but to try to fit in.

We slammed margaritas and piña coladas at Surf Bar, getting progressively louder and rowdier as the night went on. It was one of the most fun nights I'd had all summer. I was working myself to the bone, but it felt nice to have a little bit of fun, too. "God, Toronto is so boring compared to here," I said after taking a sip of my third margarita. "I don't want to go back."

"I keep forgetting you're from Canada," said Jasmine. "Though, you have a major accent."

"I do not, eh!" I said with a laugh.

"Are you French? Your last name sounds French," Jasmine continued.

"My grandpa on my dad's side is, yes," I said. "But my mom's Ojibwe. I'm also Native."

"Whoa, really?" Shelley said, joining in on the conversation while sipping one of those umbrella-clad piña coladas. "I think you're the first Native person I've ever met."

This wouldn't be the last time I heard this in New York. Indigenous people in fashion were few and far between in the Big Apple, just like they were in Toronto.

We took a hazy Uber ride home after our night out. It was well past midnight, and I was drunk and happy. Only two months in, I had already made friends *and* assisted on some of the coolest photo shoots ever. Watching the blurry Manhattan skyline zip by as we raced along the West Side Highway back to my shitty little dorm room, I cracked a little smile. New York City was where I truly belonged.

IT WAS NEARING the end of my summer *Interview* internship. I had only one week left; the summer had flown by. The last shoot I would be helping with was an all-white couture shoot, and I was packing up all the clothes. Couture is the highest calibre of clothing that fashion houses make. The pieces take months to create—all by hand, of course—and can retail for thousands (meaning, *hundreds of thousands*) of dollars. Of course, our own cultural regalia was a version of couture, taking just as long to make—it was just not as widely celebrated.

I had never seen (or touched) such expensive clothing in my

life. The fashion closet was packed to the brim with couture gems—including a dramatic Alexander McQueen caged face mask that had just gone down the runway. (When nobody was looking, a few of us interns tried on the priceless piece, snapping cheeky selfies in it.)

Midway through our work packing up some of the clothes, Jessica walked into the fashion closet. She was in a particularly bitchy mood. "Ew, it stinks in here," she said dismissively. "*Somebody* needs to wear deodorant more. I'm lighting a candle." She lit up a giant Diptyque candle on her desk with a dramatic sigh. Behind her back, all of the interns had talked about how unpredictable Jessica could be; one minute she was your best friend, and the next, she could be your complete enemy. Today, she was the latter.

We got about halfway through packing up the couture samples. At the end of the day, Jessica let us all go home. "I'll lock up in here, since these pieces are *sooo* expensive," she said. It was clear she didn't trust any of us to be alone with the priceless couture.

Before we went, Jessica instructed me on how to unlock the fashion closet and gave me a set of keys. She had an appointment she needed to go to the next morning, so I would need to open everything up. I knew it would be a busy day, as the rest of the couture needed to be packed and sent out by end of the day, so I got to the office early.

Walking in with my giant iced coffee, my Earpods blasting Britney Spears, I got off the elevator and noticed the secretary wasn't at her desk as usual. *Weird*, I thought to myself as I strolled towards the fashion closet, bopping to "Toxic." I dug through my bag to fetch the closet keys and suddenly tripped on the uneven wood floor. "What the—"

The old hardwood floors in the hallway were all warped and raised—as though they had been badly water-damaged overnight. I was confused. Was there a water leak or something? Nobody was around. I tiptoed carefully towards the closet, and then noticed the bright yellow caution tape splashed across the two glass doors. *Am I being punked?*

Inside, there were two firemen (in the classic firemen get-ups) walking around surveying the crime scene: the walls were all lined with black soot, and the floors were entirely damaged. My mouth dropped to the floor. The racks of white couture were now entirely soaked in water, and some of the pristine pieces were also covered in black soot. I looked at an elegant white coat; the sleeves appeared to have burned. I'm talking *charred*.

"Ex-excuse me," I said, barely able to comprehend what I was looking at. "I'm a fashion intern who works here. What . . . what happened?"

"There was a fire in here last night," one of the firemen said, taking note of the space. "The sprinklers went off. We think it was caused by a candle."

You mean, the candle Jessica had lit because she thought the interns "smelled"?

I immediately texted all of the interns in our group chat. "Guys," I wrote. "The closet caught on fire last night. SOS!!!"

About half an hour later, a few of the other interns started trickling in, and I debriefed them on what had happened. "Oh, my, god," said Shelley, taking off her fabulous Chanel sunglasses.

She was just as stunned as I was. "Jessica's going to *flip out*. Where is she?"

I had tried texting and calling Jessica all morning, with no reply. But a few minutes later, she walked into the office. In tears. She had clearly already received a phone call from the higher-ups.

"I'm so fired," Jessica said half laughing, half crying. "I think I forgot to blow out the candle last night."

And just like that, my *Interview* internship came to a close. It was the most dramatic ending to an already dramatic summer, which had burned as bright and fast as that Diptyque candle.

I flew back to Toronto for my last year of school and kept in touch with my core crew of intern friends. Post-closet fire, they told me that many luxury brands were now refusing to loan to *Interview*. The magazine was, for the moment, blacklisted in fashion. The whole experience was so utterly preposterous—so incredibly unbelievable, yet comical—that I still wonder if parts of it were real or a fever dream.

The New York fashion world, I realized, was batshit crazy. A place where the impossible or the most outlandish of occurrences can happen, always when you least expect it.

And I was totally hooked and wanted more.

CHAPTER 8

ZHAAYAAN NAKE
WAA-ZHI-BMAADZIYAN
(PURSUING THE WAY OF LIFE I WANT)

AFTER MY SUMMER AT *INTERVIEW*, coming back to Toronto felt like a prison sentence.

Compared to the thrilling, fast-paced season I had experienced while infiltrating New York City's fashion industry, the scene in Toronto felt dull. I had been feeling that way before I left, of course. But my feelings of melancholia were exasperated once I returned. Sure, my brief time at *Interview* was wild and crazy—definitely not normal—but the local magazines I'd once dreamed of working for, like *Flare* or *Fashion*, now felt so small-scale. So boring.

I wanted to be back in New York, shooting on set with A-list celebrities and working with fashion's top talents. A black cloud hung over my head, in a way it can only when you're a dramatic (and naive) twenty-year-old.

The final months of my last year at Ryerson dragged on. And dragged on. And *dragged* on. Time felt like it was at a standstill. I was ambitious and wanted to make a name for myself in fashion. School now felt like, frankly, a waste of time. Like it was holding me back. Whenever I wasn't doing my school assignments, I was applying to jobs back in New York, hoping I could land one as soon as I graduated, so I could book a one-way ticket and get the hell out of Toronto.

I've always been a big believer in fate and manifestation—that if you put enough good vibes and hopes and aspirations out into the world, they'll eventually come back to you. It's something my grandma used to tell me back on the rez as a kid. "*You be good now,*" she'd always say whenever we'd leave her house; I'm sure she meant to *behave,* but I always took it as a reminder to quite literally be a good person—because good things will happen to good people. If they work hard enough, that is. It's what I told myself throughout my last year in Toronto: *Just keep hustling. Something will open up for you. You'll be in New York soon enough. It's your destiny.*

You be good now.

Call it fate, but an email popped up in my inbox during one of my weekly feature writing classes. At the time, our assignment was to work on writing a heavily reported investigative feature throughout the entire semester. I was profiling an Indigenous man who'd adopted a traditional Indigenous diet and experienced a spiritual awakening as a result. I had been staring at the same story for so damn long that I was beginning to question if it was any good at all—despite the fact I had been working on it for hours and it was too late to scrap it or restart. Relieved for a tiny break, I opened the email.

It was from Mischa. She had been *Flare*'s fashion news editor during my summer internship. I had become friendly with Mischa during that time—saying the occasional "hello" and "how are you"—and I'd strategically kept in touch with her after I left, thinking she was a good contact to have on hand. *Especially* after I learned that she had moved to New York City: I needed all the contacts there that I could get.

With her blond bob and blunt-cut bangs, Mischa had a distinctive and striking look about her. She was a real fashion girl—always wearing pieces from the latest designer collections, finished off with a classic Chanel bag or sky-high stiletto. Her mother was also a prominent Canadian fashion designer, meaning she was practically *royalty* in the Toronto fashion and society scene. In New York, she was now working as the fashion editor for *Footwear News*—a sister publication to *Women's Wear Daily* that focused solely on, you guessed it: shoe news. I was curious as to why she was reaching out to little ol' me.

"Hi, Christian," Mischa wrote. "Hope you are well. We have an opening here at *Footwear News* for an assistant fashion editor. I think you should apply." *Squeal!*

At *Flare*, we had talked about my desire to eventually move to New York City. I thought it was sweet that she remembered—let alone thought of me to work as her assistant. "Send me your resumé, and I can pass it along to human resources with a recommendation," she continued. "I think you would be perfect for this."

I was thrilled at this new job prospect—though a little hesitant, too. Was working as a shoe editor my dream job in life?

Hell no. I definitely hadn't grown up wanting to write about footwear. I also felt the magazine was, well, a little *random*. However, it was owned by Condé Nast—the same company that publishes magazines such as *Vogue, Vanity Fair*, and the *New Yorker*. This entry-level job, I realized, could be my ticket into the big magazines of my dreams. My gleaming pathway to *Vogue*.

The company's human resources department asked me to interview in New York at the beginning of May—the very same month I was set to graduate from Ryerson. *I was thrilled*. At the time, the Condé Nast headquarters were located right in the heart of Times Square—a rough location for such a glamorous, glossy company. The idea of interviewing there, in the heart of the chaotic city, felt like a scene out of a movie.

I flew down to New York in May and arrived for my interview right on time—bypassing the crowds of buskers or people dressed up as Elmo for cash. The Condé Nast skyscraper had black town cars lined up outside of it—all reserved for the company's important CEOs or editor-in-chiefs, I imagined. It all felt so chic and glamorous. Moments before I walked in, I wondered if I would spot Anna Wintour leaving—*Vogue*'s editor-in-chief, who essentially rules the fashion industry.

My first meeting of the day was with a human resources manager, so I could get a general sense of the role and the company, and they could get a handle on my experience. Blah, blah, blah. *Boring*. Then I was told I'd be interviewing with two editors at *Footwear News*—Mischa and Nelson, the executive editor— at the magazine's offices, which were located just a few blocks west from the main Condé Nast headquarters in Times Square. This second interview made me nervous.

"Christian!" Mischa greeted me in the lobby. It was a standard office building, not nearly as chic as the Times Square headquarters. She looked just as fabulous as I remembered her, wearing a chic black blazer and Alaïa miniskirt. We grabbed a quick coffee and caught up, and she prepared me for my big interview with Nelson. "He's a bit of a ball-buster, but don't be nervous," she warned me, "or he'll sense it."

Nelson greeted me in a humdrum office boardroom upstairs and, despite Mischa's warning, I suddenly felt very nervous. Like, so nervous that my hands were shaking while I attempted to drink water. "So, which shoe brands do you think are dominating the market right now?" Nelson asked, instantly quizzing me on my footwear knowledge. I drew a total blank.

Shoes, I thought to myself. *Think of a fucking shoe!*

"I really like Nike," I stumbled. "I think they're really leading the sportswear space."

Sports? *You don't even watch sports, Christian!*

"Oh yeah?" Nelson asked. "You're a big fan of sports?"

"Yes, of course," I lied. My knowledge of the sports world was limited to who performed at the Super Bowl halftime show every year.

"What's your favourite sports team playing right now?"

I was way too deep into my white lie now—there was no turning back—but I couldn't think of a single team. Not one. I looked at him with a blank stare. I stumbled through a few more questions—*fashion* questions, finally—and Nelson thanked me for coming in, finally putting me out of my misery.

Well shit, I thought as I left. *I totally bombed that interview.*

A week later, I was back in Toronto to finish up my last month of school, and I was anxiously anticipating the feedback from my job interview. I expected the worst, and was preparing myself for the eventual rejection letter. I was back in my feature writing class when I got the surprising email: I had gotten the job!

"Nelson said you seemed incredibly nervous during your interview," Mischa wrote, "but he believes in your talent. Congratulations!" I couldn't focus for the rest of class; my attention was only on the exciting opportunities ahead. "One thing, though," Mischa wrote. "Please don't tell anyone you're only twenty. Let's keep that between us."

I *was* only twenty—a baby, really—but I had just scored my first big fashion job in New York City. The salary, I learned, was a measly $35,000—a barely livable wage in one of the world's most expensive cities. But I was ready to hustle and work my way up the ladder. This was my first big break, and I felt fortunate to have a job lined up right out of school. I thought about how so many of my professors had given me shit for interning on the side, telling me that my work experience was "interfering with my course load." But would I have even gotten this job, or *any* job, post-graduation if I had listened to their advice? I'm not saying one should skip school. What I am saying is it took more than good grades to land my first gig. I secured this job on my own, thanks to my own hustling.

My start date was May 27, which was the same week as my school graduation. I would have to miss it. There would be no cap-and-gown photo op for me. I didn't care, though. My new job was way more exciting. I wondered what my first day would entail.

"Your first assignment will be assisting me on a cover shoot with the designer John Varvatos," Misha emailed me. *How fabulous.*

WITH MY BIG move to New York City imminent, I needed to find a place to live. My parents and I devised a quick plan: we would fly down to New York for a weekend and line up a bunch of apartment rental viewings in the hopes of securing one then and there. I scoured apartment listings online and cold-emailed a ton of real estate agents with the same sob story, about how I was in town for one weekend and needed to find something quick. A nice blond lady named Anya with a friendly head-shot finally replied, agreeing to help me find a place. "I would suggest looking in the Upper East Side," she told us over the phone. "It's one of the more affordable neighbourhoods in the city; a lot of students and families live there. It's where I happen to live, too."

Our whirlwind weekend in New York was like an episode of *House Hunters*. Dad, Mom, and I toured a handful of apartments all in the Upper East Side. The first apartment we viewed looked like a potential crime scene. It was situated on the ground floor and featured a gigantic window looking out onto the street. The window was encased in awful, cage-like fencing. Without curtains, anybody could peep into it—a serial killer's dream. The whole studio apartment was about the size of a bedroom. You could fit a tiny twin bed, which would be just inches away from the built-in kitchen, if you could call it that: there was a fridge, stove, and sink—no counter space. In the tiny bathroom, you could not actually close the door if you were sitting on the toilet. "Absolutely not," my mom said as she looked around the place in disgust. "*This* is $1,700 a month?"

Next, we toured a slightly more expensive studio space, just a few blocks down. This one had an elevator(!), and a separate kitchen at least. Things were looking up! "To be fully transparent," our realtor Anya said as we walked around the space, "the elevator is old, and it sometimes doesn't work." The studio was on the seventh floor. *Next!*

After a few more mediocre tours, we arrived at our final viewing—a studio apartment located on Eighty-Third Street. We were beginning to lose hope in the process. The quiet street was lined with trees and looked quite pretty. The apartment was located on the third floor of a walk-up—*manageable*, I thought—and it featured two tall windows looking out onto the street. One of the windows even had a fire escape on it, and I had always romanticized the idea of sitting on one—like I was a character in *Rent* or something. The main living space was just big enough for a bed, couch, and dining table; the kitchen and bathroom were at the other end of a small hallway. The apartment was small, yes, but it was livable and actually pretty well laid-out. Plus, the kitchen had just been renovated—a rarity in Manhattan real estate.

My parents and I instantly agreed: this one felt like a home.

We filled out the forms and rental application on the spot. But because I didn't yet have a credit score in the United States, our realtor informed us that we would have to pay additional months' rent up front in order to secure it (something that is most definitely illegal now). "How many months?" my dad asked, annoyed. "This particular co-op building is asking for six months," Anya said. That was just over $10,000.

I felt horrible—guilty that my parents would have to fork up such a hefty cheque for my silly little fashion dreams to come true. For a moment, their shocked faces sent me into a tailspin;

I wondered if my dreams in New York City might not be possible after all. But my parents obliged, pulling from their own savings to do this for me. It was a pivotal moment, one that made me realize just how privileged I was. No, I didn't have a big trust fund—but my parents were willing to invest in my future, and at a heavy personal cost.

Thank you, I told them as they signed their hard-earned savings away. *Miigwetch.*

BACK AT HOME, my parents hosted a backyard family barbeque in my honour—a half–graduation celebration, half–going away party of sorts. It was a nice, sunny spring day, and the temperature was finally getting warm. All my cousins and aunts and uncles showed up to have some food and a final visit before I was off to the Big Apple.

With eighteen siblings in the mix, my mom's side of the family is full of personalities, conflicts, and craziness. But if they do one thing right, it's that they *always* show up for each other, no matter what the current circumstances and vibes are. My grandma and grandpa on my dad's side even showed up for the send-off, too. It was a rare sight to see both sides of my parents' families mix and mingle. (Let's face it, Indigenous folks and French-Italian folks don't have a ton in common.) But this was a special occasion, and I certainly felt the love from both sides that afternoon.

The elaborate spread of food—as is the tradition with our family gatherings—was big and delicious. On deck were tons of bannock (made by my auntie Joanne, who makes the *best* bannock) and all of the fixings for Indian tacos. My dad barbequed some hot dogs and burgers; my auntie Lola made one of her delicious cakes. "Good luck, Christian!" the frosted message read. We all dug in after popping some champagne.

My imminent departure—the one I had dreamed of since I was a kid—suddenly felt very real. Looking around at my big, beautiful, chaotic family, I wondered how I would fare in a city so far away from my roots. Toronto had been a culture shock, for sure, but I was always only a few hours away from home; New York was in another country, a whole other playing field—a place where there was no bannock or Indian tacos to be had. I ate a few extra pieces of bannock that day, knowing damn well that it would be a good long while before I would have some again.

I TOUCHED DOWN in New York City a week before I was to start work at *Footwear News*. I arrived with nothing but excitement and a bevy of clothes—two giant suitcases that exceeded the plane's weight limit. (Hey, I was starting a job as an assistant fashion editor: clothes were the number-one priority in my eyes.) My Upper East Side apartment wouldn't be ready to move into until the week *after* I started the job, meaning I was going to be without a home for a week. My parents decided it would be best for me to stay at a hotel until then, and the W Hotel in Times Square so happened to be having a massive discount sale. Meaning, honey, I was home!

I landed at LaGuardia Airport and lugged my hefty suitcases into a yellow taxi. Seeing the Manhattan skyline come up in the distance as we drove into the city felt so cheesy and clichéd, but I loved it. We swerved through the midtown traffic—there was honking, yelling, *chaos*—and the cab dropped me off in the heart of Times Square, just in front of the hotel. It was an odd feeling—that my first day as a New Yorker involved me living in Times Square, a neighbourhood that most real New Yorkers avoid like the plague. But the city's energy was palpable. I checked into the hotel (and my admittedly swanky room) and texted my parents that I had arrived safely in one piece. Here I was, a twenty-year-old, now living in New York City, casually ordering room service for dinner. (A burger, obviously.) *This was the life.*

I woke up for my first day at *Footwear News* extra early, clicking the button on the side of my bed so that the blackout blinds would dramatically rise. (I'm telling you; this hotel room was unnecessarily boujee!) I picked out a sleek, all-black outfit, but decided on a statement shoe—given it was my first day as a shoe editor. I rocked a pair of brown Lanvin sneakers that I had scored at Barneys—80 percent off—on my last trip.

The office was only a short fifteen-minute walk from the hotel, so I wanted to allow myself some time to get a coffee, walk and explore, and arrive to work on time. I strolled past the big, flashy Times Square billboard advertisements; the hot dog and pretzel stands; the piles of grotesque street garbage. I walked farther east and meandered through Grand Central, looking up to admire the terminal's Beaux-Arts architecture. The commute to work felt cinematic—Madonna's "Vogue" should've been the soundtrack.

I finally arrived at the *Footwear News* office building. It was located in Midtown East, a sort of dead zone in Manhattan, except for office buildings. I met Mischa in the lobby, and she escorted me up to tour the office. The space was nice enough.

There were rows of large, spacious cubicles. Maxwell, the magazine's editor-in-chief, had a large office at the back of the room. I noticed his assistant, a friendly ginger-haired woman named Cindy, planted at her desk located just in front of his door—like a guard. (If you wanted to talk to Maxwell, you had to go through her first.)

The fashion closet, where we'd be keeping the clothing and shoe samples for photo shoots, was large and had a desk and chairs in it. I learned that the *Footwear News* fashion department consisted only of Mischa and myself, so the closet was our own private little space. Mischa's job was to spearhead the fashion editorials, style the magazine's cover stars, and write trend stories or profiles. As her assistant, I would be doing all this, too—just on a lower level. My main job was to assist Mischa with whatever she needed, whether they be personal or job-related tasks.

That first week flew by, and I quickly picked up my new job routine. More often than not, Mischa and I started our day at market appointments, where you visit designer showrooms and preview a brand's or designer's new collections. This meant that we looked at hundreds—no, *thousands*—of shoes over the course of a year, so that we could see what was trending or new in the shoe space. This was also a great way to explore the city: we travelled across town for appointments, from the cool new shoe brands downtown to the veteran labels (Manolo Blahnik, Christian Louboutin) uptown. It all felt so grand and glamorous—exactly how I'd envisioned myself taking over New York.

During the rest of the day at the office, we'd work on our various fashion shoots or features for the magazine, which came out in print weekly and in digital form daily. It was all so fast-paced and fun. I was in the thick of the Manhattan fashion world.

My second week in New York, however, was far less glamorous. The time came to finally leave my plush hotel digs and move into my Upper East Side apartment. I picked up my keys from my landlord uptown—an older Polish man with a thick, gruff accent—and then grabbed my two suitcases from back at the hotel. My cab took us uptown via the Park Avenue route, and I admired all of the fancy doorman buildings along the way. *One day*, I thought. As I was unloading my two suitcases in front of my apartment, a passing dog immediately peed on one of them—his owner not even noticing. *Welcome to New York*, I thought.

I unlocked the door to my apartment. The studio was totally empty, but clean. My parents had bought me an air mattress—which took up the majority of one of my suitcases—so that I could sleep on something while I slowly began to furnish the space. When I went to inflate the mattress, I realized there was no power in the apartment. *Shit*.

I texted my landlord, who informed me that I would need to set up my own hydro with Con Edison. (I had been told this upon signing but had forgotten during my busy first week at work.) I called the utility company and was told they could come only at the end of the week. *Great*. I'd be living in the Stone Ages for a full work week.

I proceeded to hustle to and from the office that week, arriving back to a powerless, dark apartment. But I got creative. I ran an orange extension cord from a hallway outlet to inside my apartment, for whenever I needed to charge my phone or reinflate my bed—leaving my door permanently half-open in the process. You know, *very safe*. I didn't have any lamps or lighting yet, so at night, my studio was illuminated by the light of my phone screen—or a tiny solar-powered lantern I had picked up at Bed Bath & Beyond. Frat boys in college lived in better conditions than this. But to me, it all was part of the New York experience. Just like when I spotted my first cockroach.

MISCHA AND I were a fashion dream team at *Footwear News*.

Working with small budgets and tight time constraints— sometimes, we'd put together whole fashion shoots in less than a week—we became a dynamic duo. She would think of the shoot concepts (a boots shoot, a sandals shoot!), and I'd be responsible for going out to brands and calling in products for it. This meant I quickly amassed a long list of contacts at every fashion brand out there; I suddenly knew everyone in fashion, whether they were representing Gucci or Prada. I felt *in the know*.

As we continued to beef up *Footwear News*'s fashion credi- bility, our shoots got bigger and better. Mischa's eye as an edi- tor was undoubtedly good, and my taste level for what pieces we would shoot was—if I say so myself—just as good. Brands that had never heard of *Footwear News* were suddenly pitching us stories or samples to shoot; they *wanted* to be in the maga- zine. And soon, so did celebrities.

At the time, celebrity fashion lines were all the rage, and this trend was beginning to expand into the shoe world. Every star had some sort of shoe deal going on, whether it was their own footwear line or a collaboration. Mischa and I quickly began booking big-time celebrities for our covers as a result. It was a win-win on both sides, really, given that they got to promote their shoe brands (free advertising!) and we got some buzzy A-list talent. We began shooting rappers, actors, singers, you name it. Here I was, a small-town rez kid, now working with celebrities and shooting them for magazine covers. Casual.

I was particularly star-struck when I learned we would be photographing and interviewing one of the biggest pop stars *in the world*, who, at the time, had just launched her own whimsical shoe line. I had religiously listened to this pop star throughout high school; I couldn't believe I'd now be working with her. The shoot concept was simple enough: we would meet her and her team at the shoe brand's headquarters, and then photograph her with her new collection.

Mischa and I arrived a tad late—having accidentally gone to a wrong address in our Uber!—but the pop star was still getting her makeup touched up when we arrived. She looked utterly fabulous, wearing a long leopard-print dress with an extra-high ponytail. "Hi!" she greeted us. We quickly chit-chatted about our vision for the cover and how she got into shoe design, and she asked us about the magazine and how long we had worked there. I was mostly a mute—too shy to engage in conversation with someone I idolized so much. We got a photograph together. *Wow*, I thought to myself. *She's so nice!*

"Okay, I'm going to need everyone to leave the room, except for the photographer," the pop star's manager suddenly told to us. "The shoot will be just the two of them."

We were being kicked out of our own fashion photo shoot.

It wasn't our first time dealing with diva celebrity demands.

A few months later, Mischa and I were tasked with another celebrity cover shoot—photographing a male pop singer in the season's hottest men's shoes. This singer had just launched his very own (somewhat gauche) shoe line, and he wanted to promote it as part of the story. Mischa had just begun giving me more responsibility at work, so I was tasked with styling him for the editorial. I pulled out all the stops, bringing in fresh-off-the-runway pieces from labels such as Dior, Fendi, Louis Vuitton, and more.

The shoot went smashingly well. We got cool black-and-white studio images of the star rocking a handful of different shoes, while jumping in the air or doing cool body twists. While his team packed up at the end of the day, I went to check in on the star and say our goodbyes—only to be told he had already left the building. He had already left the building wearing one of the total looks that I had pulled *from the runway*, to be specific. A look from a *very* expensive brand that needed that look back tomorrow morning.

We had a runaway fashion thief on our hands!

They say fashion is glamorous, but nobody tells you about the part where a fashion assistant has to spend more than twenty-four hours chasing down a celebrity to retrieve a stolen outfit. I learned that, in this industry, you should trust nobody—not even the stars. Perhaps *especially* not the stars. But I was persistent, and after tracking down the star's assistant, hotel, *and* schedule, I ordered his assistant to get him to give the outfit back. And he did.

Don't mess with a rez kid.

THERE *WERE* GLAMOROUS moments, however, during my days as a shoe editor. The best part about my job was the travel: we'd often fly to Las Vegas, Miami, the Hamptons, California, or even Nashville for our photo shoots. In one work year, I had travelled to more places than I had in my entire life. As a treat for all my hard work, I even got to attend Milan Fashion Week every season as well, to report on the menswear shows.

During my first trip to Milan, I didn't know what to expect. I had never been to Europe before. My grandmother on my dad's side, Laura, had immigrated to Canada from Fano, Italy; I immediately felt a sense of closeness to that heritage and side of my family. But Europe has a, well, *complicated* relationship with Indigenous people; I also felt a sense of power in being a Native person touching down in Milan and schmoozing with the Italian fashion crowd. Almost like I was conquering a piece of their territory, for once.

Footwear News's parent company, Condé Nast, had a satellite office in Milan, which is where I would be working for the week. The office was shared between *Footwear News* and *Women's Wear Daily*—sister magazines that, weirdly enough, could get very competitive with each other. The team at *WWD* was made up of veteran fashion journalists who had been with the publication for years, if not decades. This meant many of them were surly, or jaded. I was a young twentysomething fresh on the scene in Milan—so they, naturally, chose to never acknowledge my existence.

During my whole week at the Milan office, the *WWD* team barely spoke to me. On my first day of the Milan shows, I was wearing my new Prada sweater (which I had gotten on sale) with my favourite Prada shoes (which I'd also gotten on sale). "*Someone* loves Prada," the *WWD* fashion director said snidely, giving my outfit the up-and-down. Fashion people could be such bitches. Between the shows, we were all supposed to share a town car—but there were multiple times when the *WWD* team left me behind after the show, forcing me to Uber or find my own way to the next destination. En route to the Vivienne Westwood menswear show, my Italian taxi driver even hit a cyclist. Neither of them spoke English, but the injured cyclist did give me a thumbs-up to communicate he was okay. *Stai bene?* I kept asking, with a crazed look on my face. *Are you okay?!*

There was definitely an air of pettiness around the office, but I didn't care. I was reporting in Milan! I couldn't have been happier. When I wasn't writing about the runway shows or shoe trends of the season, I made time to go see the Duomo di Milano—a massive, Gothic-style cathedral right in the heart of the city, just steps away from the office. I climbed the treacherous stairs, overly dressed but wearing my comfortable dress shoes, determined to get a view from the top. It was stunning—a panoramic view of the city. I'm glad I made time to enjoy this touristy experience. Afterwards, I ate the best pizza I've ever had at a place just around the corner.

At the shows, I couldn't believe I had seats at some of the most prestigious fashion shows in the world. My first Prada show—my favourite fashion brand—was especially a highlight. It was their spring 2018 season, and legendary designer Miuccia Prada cited comic books as a major inspiration for the collection. The whole venue was covered in pop art–style graphics, and the clothes had strips of comic art on the techy zip-up jackets or pinstriped shirts. I was in awe of what was coming down the runway: it felt both traditional and super contemporary. It was beautiful. When Miuccia came out to do her shy bow, just steps away from my seat, my eyes even watered. I felt so lucky.

I didn't know many people in Milan, but luckily, there were a few shoe designers I'd met back in New York who took me under their wing. Giovanni was an Italian shoe designer who had a line of playful, eccentric women's shoes. I spotted him at the Missoni show and was so glad to see a familiar face—especially after a few days of being treated like I had the plague by my *WWD* co-workers. Afterwards, he invited me to a Fashion Week party with him and some of his (gorgeous) Italian friends.

Sì!

The party was in an old, cavernous building where there was loud, thumping Italian pop playing, everyone looked like a model (even the waiters were hot), and the Aperol spritz cocktails were flowing. I felt a dash of imposter syndrome in that moment—how had a kid from Nipissing First Nation ended up here?—but I played along and acted cool.

Drinking several Aperol spritzes is an easy way lose any and all inhibitions, though, and I proceed to do just that. Giovanni introduced me to all of his cool Italian friends, some of whom didn't speak a word of English, and our group got to dancing. In our crew was a model-looking guy who resembled a young Elvis Presley. He spoke broken English, smelled of cigarettes, and had great hair and big biceps. I blame the Aperol spritz, but I ended the night by making out with him.

Welcome to Milan, he managed to say as we parted ways.

If this is what the Italians meant by *la dolce vita*, then I was definitely living it. Working in fashion seemed like everything I'd hoped it would be.

But that feeling didn't last long.

CHAPTER 9

MAJI-MSHKIKI
(BAD MEDICINE)

MY THREE YEARS AT *FOOTWEAR News* served as an intensive crash course in what the real fashion industry was all about. And I was learning that it wasn't for the weak.

Back in New York, Mischa and I were still grinding away in the office on our fashion shoots. Every week, we had to produce a brand new layout for the magazine. There were western boot shoots, photographed in a country bar in Nashville; rain boot shoots, where we repeatedly sprayed buckets of water over a poor model to achieve that "wet look"; kids' footwear shoots, where we'd attempt to wrangle infant models on set. We once even shot a pair of bunny-ear sneakers next to a real-life bunny, who had his very own handler. There was no shoot concept that was too wild or wacky for us to try.

Shooting editorials every week meant that Mischa and I worked on a very fast-paced schedule—there was never really a moment of rest. When one shoot ended, there was another one to begin. Whether we were conceptualizing ideas, calling in clothes or shoes, reviewing models, or scouting locations, we were a dynamic duo that was always—*always*—busy. Somehow, we made up the magazine's entire fashion department (typically, the fashion team has *way* more than two people).

I loved the chaotic nature of the job—at first. But the work was far from glamorous. Most days, you'd find me hiding out in the fashion closet and unpacking bags and bags of shoes. Not only did I have to source and call in products, liaising with various brands' PR contacts, but I had to physically unpack and organize them all in the closet. On shoot day, I'd arrive extra early and start packing everything—then proceed to haul it to the location, unpack it, and do it all over in reverse when the shoot was over.

On set, I was also the errand boy—the bitch boy, basically—running out to get anything and everything we needed for the shoot (oftentimes, it was a pack of cigarettes for the moody photographer). On one particularly exhausting shoot day, Mischa even asked me to take her English bulldog puppy—a stocky little boy who did *not* enjoy my company—to a routine vet appointment. Only, he barked at me so ferociously when we tried to get into the Uber that Mischa had to take him herself while I ran the shoot.

I understood that, in fashion, working your way up was a necessary evil. I wasn't going to be spearheading shoots like Mischa was overnight! I knew I had to pay my dues. But I had been interning since I was nineteen years old, and doing such grunt work in my mid-twenties was starting to get old. I began to feel creatively stuck. There are only so many shoes you can pack and unpack before things start to feel repetitive.

I also began fearing that I'd be stuck working as a shoe editor forever. I desperately wanted to work in fashion on a much larger scale—at a much bigger magazine—where I could write or shoot any aspect of fashion I wanted to. I felt like my talents were being caged. I did not want to write about footwear for the rest of my life.

MISCHA AND I were busy working on our latest photo shoot for the "sneakerhead" issue—one of *Footwear News*'s biggest issues of the year, where we spotlight the coolest and newest sneakers on the market. As usual, my job was to call in all of the sneaker samples (men's and women's) that we were going to photograph in an edgy still-life editorial. Hundreds of emails later, the fashion closet had filled up with top-of-the-line sneakers. There were sporty Adidas and Nike styles, as well as sleek designer styles from Giuseppe Zanotti and Christian Louboutin. It was a sneaker lover's fever dream: there was thousands and thousands of dollars' worth of product in there.

After the shoot was over, I was back in the fashion closet, packing up all of the shoes into shopping bags. It was an all-too-familiar routine. I methodically taped up each bag, labelled them one by one, and then brought all the hefty shopping bags down to our mail room, where the brand messengers would come to pick them up. *I'm sick of this grunt work*, I grumbled to myself, hauling the bags to the mail room.

The next day, back at my desk, I received an email with an urgent subject line.

"URGENT: MISSING SHOES!!"

It was from a luxury shoe brand that had loaned us several sneakers for the shoot. I read the email carefully. The brand claimed they had yet to receive their four shopping bags of sneakers back. *That's odd*, I thought. *I packed those up yesterday.*

I double-checked our messenger log. It said that the four shopping bags had indeed been picked up and delivered back to the brand. I called the messenger service and asked them to confirm delivery. "Yes, they were delivered yesterday," a customer service rep told me. The brand still insisted they hadn't arrived. *Something wasn't adding up.*

I went into Mischa's office and explained the situation, knowing how serious it was. "If we can't locate the missing sneakers," she said, "the magazine will have to pay the brand thousands of dollars for those lost samples." My heart was racing; I *had* to find the missing shoes. I could get fired for this!

I started by contacting our building's security department, asking if there were cameras or tapes I could review—like I was an FBI agent or something. I then called my parents on my lunch break, explaining the situation while fighting back tears. "It's just shoes," my mom said on the other end of the line. Really, *really fucking expensive* shoes, I reminded her.

It took two weeks for our security department to review the camera recordings. In the meantime, the brand emailed me almost every single day, putting more and more pressure on me to find the bags. I began to lose sleep over the matter. The higher-up bosses at *Footwear News* also questioned me constantly about the situation, almost as though I had stolen them or misplaced them myself. I felt unsupported and, frankly, ganged up on. And then one Thursday afternoon, the case was solved: a messenger had been filmed on camera picking up the bags, but he'd never delivered them. It was a classic case of robbery.

Sure, working in fashion had its glamorous moments, but I was learning (the hard way) that behind the scenes, folks working in the industry (like me) were grinding away and subject to anything *but* glamour. You may dream of styling photo shoots and working with cool models and hair stylists and makeup artists—but realistically, you may spend weeks of your life investigating a sneaker robbery you never asked for.

I was starting to wonder: Did I really care about fashion *enough* to put up with this?

My time at *Footwear News* took a turn for the worse when the company decided to hire a new digital director. It sounds archaic now, but at the time, digital journalism was only just finding its footing in the fashion industry. The magazine was beginning to ramp up the number of digital stories and amount of web content that it produced. This meant that, in addition to my regular job duties for the print magazine—all those photo shoots each month!—I now had daily web assignments and write-ups to do, too.

The new digital director was—how can I put this nicely?—a terror. The previous web editor was a friendly woman named Mandy from Australia who was bubbly and a great team player. The new digital director was all business and numbers, and treated the writers on staff like they were robots who could—no, *must*—fill their quotas. They were so awful to work with that I even developed a not-so-kind nickname for them, which I often used while complaining to friends.

The Web Dictator messaged me at all hours of the day. Often, with the same exact line: "Please write this up." In the office, they would direct-message me over Slack, even though they were sitting just a few feet away. When we did speak in person, they refused to look me in the eye, as though my physical presence as a human didn't exist.

Unfortunately, sometimes you have to work with people you may find it difficult, or impossible, to work with. You might even have to report to them. I knew this was a reality, but I had never once worked for someone so difficult—and I was struggling to make it work. I started resenting the job, which I already felt was holding me back from the brighter future I knew I deserved. As a naive person in their twenties, my first thought went immediately to the dramatic: What if I just quit, and walked out the door?

I was now three years into my life in New York City, and what had once been my dream job was now turning into a nightmare. Something had to change.

OUTSIDE OF WORK, I relied on my friends in the city to help me cope with it all.

That support system was essential. My friends helped me to blow off steam and have some *fun*. It hadn't taken long for me to reconnect with some of the fashion folks I had met while interning at *Interview* back in university. One of my closest friends in the city was Jasmine, who had been the head intern at *Interview* during my summer there. We hung out non-stop: she was my main fashion friend.

Jasmine was now working as a fashion editor for *Elle*, so we would often go to work events together and then grab dinner and drinks afterwards. It felt good to have a friend in the industry, someone to share common struggles and commiserate with. (She had her own share of demanding bosses.) We got along so well because we loved fashion, and we *loved* shopping and going out. We spoke the same language—the language of being an underpaid fashion writer trying to make it in New York City.

During our many happy-hour chats, we'd talk about who we were dating, or what was going on at work. Lately, I'd begun complaining more and more about feeling stuck in my job. "You need to quit already," she'd always say. I began to worry that I might never work for a *real* fashion magazine. I hid it well, but I was really becoming depressed.

And like unhappy people often do, I began to self-medicate. With alcohol. *Lots* and lots of alcohol. And sometimes drugs, too.

It was a particularly nice summer Thursday night in the city, and I had just wrapped up another hellish work week. I got a text from Jasmine: "Wanna go out in Brooklyn tonight?" *Duh.* It wasn't even a question. Everybody in New York knows that Thursday is the new Friday.

My mission for the night was loud and clear: to drink until I was belligerent. Before hitting the bars, there was always a pre-game at Jasmine's apartment. I downed a whole bottle of white wine like it was nothing, and took a few tequila shots, too. Why not? My aim was to be drunk before even hitting the streets. Sober, I felt overworked and stuck in my job—but with a few drinks in me, I forgot all about my career unhappiness. A cheap pinot grigio offered instant escape.

When you're in your twenties, drinking a lot doesn't necessarily seem like a red flag. It's what you do to be social—you hit the bars with your friends! But my indulgent tendencies began to grow more and more out of control, a process that happened slowly until—one day—I was as dependent on alcohol as I was on water.

Pretty much every single night after work, I'd have the same crippling thought. *I desperately need a drink.* Not just *a* drink—several drinks. My fridge at home had a constant rotation of white wine bottles in it, awaiting me like old friends. I'd almost always polish off a bottle a night. And when I was hitting the town, those drinks at home were just the appetizer.

Jasmine and I decided to hit up a few of our favourite haunts in Brooklyn. There was Pete's Candy Store, a small dive bar that had a cool live music venue in the back room. Sometimes the bands were amazing; other times they were a total flop. But more importantly, the drinks were good and *cheap*. We ordered several tequila sodas while we watched an ethereal folk band bang around some tambourines.

Then onto the next spot. With a slight buzz going, we hit up a dance bar that we could never remember the name of. It was underneath a highway bridge, and they played *great* music. We ordered several more tequila sodas, and we danced to the new Drake album, played at an ear-splitting volume. The room began to pulsate. Throb. *Spin.*

Fade to black.

I came to in the back of an Uber, thrust awake by the feeling that I was about to vomit. *How did I get here? When did I leave the bar?* Before I could answer these questions, I was projectile vomiting all over the backseat of the Honda Civic.

"Get the fuck out!" screamed my Uber driver. My Uber rating had for sure just plummeted.

Embarrassed, I stumbled out of the Uber and tried to get a grasp on where the hell I was. *Park Avenue.* Okay, at least I was back in my Upper East Side neighbourhood. My phone was about to die, but I drunkenly attempted to get my bearings and Google-Map my journey home. Thankfully, home was only ten minutes away. I was definitely way too drunk to call another Uber, and I didn't think I could stomach another car ride, either. I was just going to have to walk home, covered in puke.

As I stumbled my way east towards home, I suddenly had a very desperate need to pee. I began walking a little faster. *Did Jasmine get home safely?* I couldn't remember anything after the dancing. The fact that my bladder was about to burst didn't help. I made it to just a few feet outside of my apartment, *dying* to use the bathroom, when I realized that I couldn't find my keys. I dumped my bag out on the sidewalk, desperately scrounging for my keys on the ground while I swayed from side to side.

"Fuck, where are my KEYS?"

Suddenly, I felt a sense of warmth along my right leg. I was pissing myself. It was the middle of the night, and I was now covered in vomit *and* urine. I began sobbing uncontrollably. There was nobody around to witness it, except a fat rat that scurried by.

I woke up the next morning to the sound of birds chirping.

For a split second, it was a rather pleasant wake-up call—until a terrible smell hit me from the urine- and vomit-stained clothes that were lying in a crumpled heap next to my bed. *How lovely.*

I guess I had somehow found my keys and passed out in bed. I checked my phone for the time, only it was dead. "Shit!!" I must have forgotten to charge it when I got home. It was now Friday, and I was due at work. I didn't know the time, but I was *definitely* late. I sprang out of bed—my head throbbing, no, *pounding* with a headache—and plugged my phone in to check the time. It was almost noon.

Once my phone powered up, the flurry of text messages started to come in one by one.

"Are you OK???"

"Christian, where are you?"

"Please call me."

Several of my co-workers had tried calling and texting multiple times in the morning, after I didn't show up to work. They were convinced I had died. It happened to be an important day in the office: I was needed in the fashion closet to work on a major celebrity cover shoot. Who else could unpack and organize all of the incoming clothes and shoes? I instantly called Mischa in a panic. "I'm so sorry, I overslept. I will be right there," I said in a gravelly tone, my voice breaking on every second word. I felt ill. I haphazardly cleaned myself up, threw on some fresh clothes, and ran out the door—looking like as much of a hot mess as you'd imagine.

I reeked of tequila; it was oozing out of my pores. I ran out the door of my apartment and headed to the subway. *I should not have done those shots,* I thought to myself as I fought back more puke on the train. I got a text from Jasmine that she was alive, *thank god*, and that she also didn't remember getting home. We had clearly overdone it.

When I showed up at the office, I was very much still drunk. My hazy vision made everything seem like it was pulsating or spinning. I avoided eye contact with my co-workers as I strolled, keeping my head down as I sauntered towards my desk in shame. I could feel people's eyes burning into the back of my head, like lasers.

Sadly, it was not the first time I'd shown up for work still drunk from the night before. It was starting to become a routine—as though the only way I could cope with such a stressful job was to drink my sorrows away the night before. Mischa was, understandably, annoyed that I was so late. Though she was relieved I was okay.

"We were worried about you," she said bluntly, looking up and down at my dishevelled appearance.

I couldn't look her in the eye. "So sorry again," I said sheepishly. "I'm going down to the fashion closet and will catch up on all the samples."

I ran off to the closet to recover in peace. I puked about three more times that day.

MY BEHAVIOUR WAS out of control. I was on a rapid path towards self-destruction. I would find any and all excuses to party during the week—and in a demanding industry like fashion, it was always easy to find overworked folks who also needed a stiff drink.

A good party friend of mine was Ella, a pretty blond from the South who I had met at work. She freelanced for *Footwear*

News as a fashion assistant, helping Mischa and me on our various shoots. We instantly bonded because, well, we were both nice people working in fashion—a rarity at the time, about as rare as a unicorn sighting.

Each week, you could usually find Ella and me down at Gemma—the swanky restaurant attached to the Bowery Hotel. We frequented the spot so often during the work week that we knew every single bartender by name. They became like family to us. Often, our bill at the end of the night would be completely taken care of—thank god, as we were both broke—or we'd be charged for a single round of drinks, even though we had been served about six martinis each. God bless those men.

Another such friend was Dianne, a PR representative for a big, glamorous New York–based fashion house. We had also met working together on *Footwear News* shoots. She would loan us clothes and shoes for our editorials. Dianne and I developed an instant rapport, mostly because our jobs worked us to the bone and we loved to drink after hours. She was also from Canada, and I admired her friendly spirit. Plus, she was pretty and fashion-forward—exactly the type of person I wanted to hang with.

Dianne's office was just down the street from mine, so we would often meet up for post-work drinks in Bryant Park, a mid-point between us. Surrounded by the city's skyscrapers, we'd often down several bottles of rosé at the Bryant Park Grill—all on Dianne's corporate card (a perk of dining with PR folks). We'd talk about what was stressing us out at work; which editors we liked and disliked; what dates we had gone on; who we had just hooked up with.

I had just had my turbulent blackout night out with Jasmine

the week before, but I was raging to go out again, so I texted Dianne. It was a Friday night this time—*no work tomorrow, thank god!*—so we made plans to hit the town. "Come over to my apartment and we'll go from there," she texted me. My feet were already halfway out the door.

Dianne shared a small railroad-style apartment in Gramercy with two roommates. When I arrived, she had a full glass of wine ready for me. "My friend André is a stylist, and he's invited us over for drinks later," she said as she handed me the glass.

"I'm down!" I said, taking a big gulp of wine.

We Uber'd over to André's apartment on the Lower East Side, already a little tipsy from the cheap sauvignon blanc we'd just chugged. The hallway in André's apartment was lined with racks and racks of clothes. It was clear he was using his house as his styling studio (with Manhattan rent prices, everything works double duty). Lying around were sequined gowns, chic tailored suits, feathered cocktail dresses.

"Shots anyone?" he said.

André, Dianne, and I had tequila shots, and then drank more wine. André told us of a party that was happening at the Boom Boom Room—one of New York's hardest nightclubs to get into, at the top of the Standard Hotel. An actor he had styled for red carpets was having his birthday party there, so André invited us. "I could get you on the list, if you guys want to come," he said. Dianne and I looked at each other with a glimmer in our eyes. "*Uh, yeah we do,*" we said with a laugh.

We blasted music in the taxi on our way to the party. By the time we made it to the door and past the bouncer, we were already on the verge of blacking out. We bypassed the long line, and André escorted us up the elevator and into the club.

The space—lined with windows, looking out on the city's epic skyline—was dark and glamorous. There was a large, art deco–style bar in the middle of the room, and Dianne and I—for some very stupid reason—decided to order martinis. Because we needed them.

The music thumped. The conversations got blurry. We met the entire cast of a hit Netflix show—only, neither Dianne nor I remembered doing so the following morning. What we *do* remember was tripping several times on our way out—Dianne losing her jacket and me losing my wallet in the process—and somehow flinging ourselves into a cab home.

As we texted back and forth the following morning—me fighting back the urge to projectile vomit in bed, again—it was clear that the entire night was erased from our memories.

"What happened to you guys last night??" André texted.

We had no idea.

My excessive drinking was becoming a pattern, and it was starting to scare me. That morning, I finally said the words out loud: "You need to make a change."

WHEN MY SISTER and I were growing up, my mom had explained the teachings of the Ojibwe medicine wheel to us. The medicine wheel's four quadrants represent many different things—among them, the four directions, the four elements of the earth, and the four seasons. They also represent the four elements that are needed for a person's true well-being: a balance between the physical, intellectual, emotional, and spiritual. It teaches us that in order to live a truly balanced and harmonious life, these four elements need to always be in check:

all the elements work together and interact. If you're lacking in one, you're lacking in them all. As my mental health began to decline in New York, I realized that my medicine wheel was *all out of whack*. I needed to make a change in order for myself, and my soul, to be restored and healed.

I thought about how I'd once longed to work in New York City, how that dream had fed my soul. But now that I was here, I was angry and unhappy. I had totally lost my sense of purpose and direction in life. I felt ungrounded. Unconnected. Unfulfilled.

Part of me was acting out, of course. With the excessive partying and drinking, I secretly hoped that I would get called out on my bad behaviour. I wanted to get fired, so that I could be free from the job I felt so stuck in. I also realized that all of my partying was just a distraction. My reckless behaviour was holding me back from making a much bigger decision. Sobering up meant making a choice, making a change.

I called my mom one night after work.

"How's your week going," she asked, concerned, as she always was. "You sound tired."

"Mom, I don't think I can do this job anymore," I said bluntly, while taking a leisurely walk around the block near my apartment. A car horn blared for dramatic effect.

Mom was used to my complaining. "I'm serious," I said, fighting back tears. "I think I'm done. I haven't felt well mentally for a while now."

She took a long pause. "Well, you do have to protect your *bmaadziwin*."

In Ojibwe, we say *mino-bmaadziwin* to represent living "the good life." I was clearly lacking in this area. We talked about what my next steps would be—what I would do for money; how I would survive in an expensive city like New York while, well, jobless.

"We can figure that out," she said. "But you have to take care of yourself."

It was all I needed to hear.

The next week, I worked up the courage to give my resignation at work. And I picked the most dramatic way possible to do it, of course.

Walking into Mischa's office with the intention of resigning, I was surprised to hear she'd beat me to the punch: she shared that she had just given hers. "My husband and I will actually be relocating to Miami, and I'm pursuing freelance work," she said. I was shocked. It was another sign: if Mischa—my mentor, and one of my only work confidants—was heading out the door, there was no better time for me to bow out, too.

An hour later, I met with our editor-in-chief, Maxwell, in his office. Maxwell was a glamorous figure who knew celebrities and always floated in and out of the office. He admired my hard work, and I respected his vision for the magazine, but we rarely spoke one-on-one. He had a large office that was entirely lined with windows that looked out on Manhattan's skyline. In his large office, I felt so small—terrified about the news I was about to deliver.

"Hi, Christian, take a seat," Maxwell said. "I'm assuming you've heard about Mischa's departure. I'm assuming that's why you're here. I know you're probably wondering what's going to happen to the fashion department, now that she's leaving."

"Yes," I said. "Well, about that."

His face dropped.

"I'm sorry to do it like this, but I think I'm going to be giving my notice as well."

His face was shocked. "*Why?*" he said, clearly disappointed as he slumped in his seat.

"I think I'm at a point where I need to re-evaluate what I want to do with my career, and I need time to kind of explore that for a little bit," I said. I felt like a failure the moment the words came out of my mouth. But it was true: I was totally lost.

"We can give you a sabbatical," Maxwell said, trying to entice me to stay. "And I was planning on promoting you." This was news to me: I had been feeling totally undervalued at work. He threw out a surprisingly large salary number to make me stay, and for a second, I considered it. But he could have paid me $10,000,000 at that point and it wouldn't have been enough. I decided I was done.

"It's not about the money," I maintained. "I think I just need some time off."

I walked out of the office that day feeling a mix of emotions. I had just quit my New York dream job, and for once in life, I had no future plans. I had no clear goals lined up, no plan of attack for my next big career move. For the moment, I just wanted to *breathe*. To have no big aspirations. I realized I didn't really know much about myself outside of my work. For most of my adult life, I had let my job define me as a person. I did feel nervous about my choice, and was unsure if I had made the right decision. What if I never worked in fashion again? I didn't care. Because, for once, I felt something that I hadn't felt in a really long time: Freedom.

A freedom to reintroduce myself—to the world and, more importantly, to myself.

Walking home, I even cracked a smile, something I had not done a lot of recently.

AS I FINISHED off my last week at *Footwear News*, I started to feel sentimental about my journey at the magazine. Bored at my desk, I began scrolling back through all the work I had produced over the past three years. Lately, I had been feeling totally disengaged from what I was writing about—but there were many stories I *was* incredibly proud of, including my cover stories, for which I'd interviewed designers such as Rick Owens and Christian Louboutin, the shoe genius behind those luxurious red soles.

I also came across a story that I had written on Jamie Okuma. Jamie was an Indigenous artist who, I learned in my research, was hand-beading luxurious Christian Louboutin heels, adding a dash of cultural flair to high-end shoes. They were gorgeous to look at, sure, but I thought her work was incredibly clever. Instead of designers appropriating elements of Indigenous culture—which has been the case for years, if not *centuries*—Jamie was essentially flipping the script, and putting a Native twist on designer items. It felt like a powerful idea, using fashion to reclaim culture.

As I reread the story, I remembered how much of a success it had been. When I posted the story to the *Footwear News* website, it ended up doing amazingly well, traffic-wise, becoming one of the month's most-read pieces. That had been a surprise, as I hadn't anticipated anyone reading, let alone caring about, the story. It was the first time I realized that there was a sense of power in covering Indigenous fashion. Not only was there clearly an appetite for it, but it was also an easy and effective way to educate others about Native culture. *I want to do more of* this, I thought to myself.

I had never once really thought about writing about fashion from my own cultural point of view. I didn't think anyone cared. I had spent so long being ashamed of my Native identity—that I wasn't Native enough, didn't look Native enough—that I had wrongly assumed that nobody would consider Native culture interesting. But a tide shifted inside of me in that exact moment. *Maybe this could be my next step.*

CHAPTER 10

MKAMAAN MINO-BMAADZIWIN (FINDING A GOOD WAY OF LIFE)

"DO YOU KNOW HOW TO make a ribbon shirt?"

It was the summer of 2017. Mom and I were sitting out on the deck of my parents' house back in Canada. It's an idyllic summer spot where our family has spent many, many summer months. Their beautiful backyard, spanning almost an acre, looks out onto a river that boats and kayakers frequently pass by on. The nearby fire pit is the perfect spot to make s'mores as you wave them all by. The weather was just getting warm and glorious, and the plentiful garden was starting to bloom.

This was my first summer home since burning out and leaving my big, fancy New York fashion job. I'd decided to come home to celebrate my birthday in June—but more importantly, to escape the chaos of the city, gather my thoughts, and figure out my next move. I still had my apartment back in Manhattan, of course—I had no plans to leave the Big Apple *just yet*—but being unemployed, I figured I could at least save some cash while being home for a bit. Plus, I figured, I might as well visit some family while I'm sorting out my next chapter. After all, there's nothing like spending a few weeks back home to get your soul and spirit in order.

"Hmmm?" my mom replied from her lounge chair, lifting up her sunglasses as the sun beamed on us. We were catching some rays side by side—our mandatory Diet Cokes, with lots of ice, in hand.

"Do you or any of the aunties know how to make a ribbon shirt?" I repeated. "I've been thinking that I would like one."

I'd gotten the idea to ask her for a ribbon shirt after seeing my sister try on her traditional jingle dress. Our annual Nipissing powwow was coming up soon, and my sister was trying on some of the new beaded accessories that she'd made to go with her regalia. Her jingle dress—adorned with a rainbow assortment of colours, and lines of jingle cones—was stunning. The garment was entirely handmade and, in my opinion, rivalled some of the couture gowns I'd seen come down the high-fashion runways. It took many hands, and months, to make. And seeing it on her, I realized I didn't own a single piece of Indigenous regalia myself. It felt like it was time.

Back home in Nipissing, there were certainly no fashion shows or celebrity photo shoots, but I *was* surrounded by our own cultural style. On the rez, you often caught sight of people wearing striking ribbon skirts and shirts, hide moccasins, or beaded earrings. These were all pieces that I'd been strongly opposed to wearing as a kid, but, now that I was an adult, I began to recognize their unique beauty. I didn't own a single piece of Indigenous-made clothing—it felt like a sin!

"Yes, I think we could make you one," my mom finally replied, trying to play it cool.

I had never once asked my mom to make me a piece of Indigenous clothing as a kid. In fact, I fought against it *hard* during my bratty teenage years, convinced that wearing a ribbon shirt would somehow make me the uncoolest kid at school. I could tell by her subtle grin that she was excited I had finally asked her.

A few days later, my aunties Joanne, Lola, and Tasha all came over to the house. They were going to help my mom do the fitting for my new ribbon shirt. I knew I would get a beautifully made shirt out of the experience—I never doubted that—but what I didn't anticipate was just how special the whole design process would be.

"You first need to choose the colours of your ribbon shirt," my mom said as we all sat around the kitchen table by her sewing machine. "All of the colours in a ribbon shirt typically represent something special; they have to mean something to you."

I thought about it for a few minutes. I didn't just want to just pick my favourite colours; I wanted them to symbolize something much deeper and more personal. Then, it came to me: What if the shirt featured the favourite colours of my parents and grandparents? It would be a vibrant (and colourful!) way to pay tribute to my Elders and family lineage. We landed on the final colours together: red, yellow, black, white, and blue.

Once the array of colourful ribbons were sewn onto the shirt—first in a horizontal formation across the chest, and then with dangling vertical strips, a *very* Ojibwe style—I tried it on. My mom and aunties had me do a little twirl. "We need something on the back," my auntie Joanne said, giving it a discerning up-and-down glance.

"What about our crane crest?" my mom suggested.

In Ojibwe culture, communities are assigned to an animal clan, a *doodem*, that signifies one's responsibilities and skills. In the case of our family, we belonged to the Crane clan—a clan that represents leadership, among other qualities. Having the crane embroidered onto the back, my mom said, would be another way to represent where I'm from and the values our family and community stand for.

"I love it," I replied.

About a week later, the finished shirt came back from my aunties. A family friend embroidered the crane imagery on the back, and the shirt finally felt complete. When I slipped on the final design, I felt more than just beautiful or stylish—I felt empowered. I felt a sense of pride in being Indigenous—a feeling that, for much of my youth, had very much been a foreign concept. Away from the glitz and glamour of New York's high-fashion world, I reconnected with a different kind of fashion identity—one that felt intrinsically me. It took that moment of pause and stepping out of the New York grind to make me realize: our own Indigenous designs back home fucking *rule*!

I documented the entire design process with photos and notes, and realized just how much storytelling goes into the making of our Indigenous garments. As I was feeling creatively lost and searching for what would be next in my career, I wondered if this could be the new focus of my writing. *What if I began writing more about Indigenous fashion?*

It seemed a shame to me that nobody was writing about the beauty and thoughtfulness that goes into making Indigenous regalia—the formalwear that's worn for ceremonial or pow-wow purposes (though sometimes ribbon shirts and skirts are worn for everyday, too). Never mind that nobody was covering the talented contemporary Native artists who were carrying forward their cultural traditions through clothes. I was still jobless, but going into the summer, I was armed with something I hadn't felt in months, or maybe even years: *inspiration*. I had a drive again. A purpose to my work that I felt I had lost.

A fire was lit inside of me.

BACK IN NEW York, I began to establish a little "funemployment" routine for myself while I started to hunt for jobs. I was trying to enjoy the not-working era as much as I could—I needed the rest after a crazy few years hustling and bustling—but the crippling fear of not being able to make rent would always manage to creep its way in. However, being free to run around New York City in the summer, with no job or obligations, is a luxury few are afforded, so as I sent my resumé around town (to virtually every fashion magazine possible), I figured I might as well try to enjoy the city.

My shoebox studio apartment on the Upper East Side—which fit only a bed, a couch, and a dining table—felt especially claustrophobic if I stayed there too long, so I made it a point to get out of the house and do something every day. Sometimes, it was a walk to the nearby Metropolitan Museum of Art, where I'd spend hours walking around. (The historical Native artifacts were always a favourite, though to me many of them seemed imprisoned by the institution; they belong to their tribes!) Other times, I'd just roam the streets uptown, or go sit in Central Park and read a book. I was very much a lost soul trying to fill my time to avoid spiralling. But at the same time, I felt free; I was focusing on me.

I wasn't *totally* jobless. A Canadian children's publishing company had just approached me about writing a fashion book for young adults, and given I had nothing but time on my hands, I gladly accepted the offer. I started slowly working on the project; I wanted to expose children to the concept of cultural clothing, and how what we wear can bear special meaning beyond just the aesthetics. I wanted to teach them that one's sense of style can come with a sense of power. Often, I'd spend my days at a café writing.

It helped that my friend Dianne, who I had met at *Footwear News*, had just left her job at a big, fancy fashion house—so we were commiserating in our funemployment era. Often, we would meet up at Sheep Meadow in Central Park to grab some rays, day drink, and chit-chat about our dating life or job searches.

"What have you applied to this week?" Dianne asked as she filled my red Solo cup with more rosé. We were laying out and tanning, as usual. (My drinking was now under control; after focusing on myself and removing myself from a stressful work environment, I was able to consume alcohol on a more social level again, without binging.)

"There's an accessories job at *InStyle* that I applied for, but I haven't heard back," I replied. I was starting to feel defeated by the rejections—or, worse, by the magazines who didn't even reply to my applications, despite the fact that I was overqualified for the jobs they were posting.

"I have an interview at an accessories brand this week, actually," Dianne said. She, too, hadn't had any luck with job postings for weeks. At least one of us had a lead.

"Honestly, the only magazine I want to work at is *Vogue*," I continued, as we pondered life. "The whole reason I left my other job is because I felt stuck, right? So I'm not even going to apply to anything that doesn't feel 100 percent right."

"Cheers to that, honey," Dianne said as we knocked our cups together.

I also knew that I wanted a job where I could write about things that I cared about. I was hungry to write about Indigenous fashion, and to spotlight all of the cool artists and designers that I knew existed out there. A magazine like *Vogue* would be the perfect place to do this, I thought, given its huge audience and platform. I wanted to introduce Indigenous culture to a whole new readership. And in the biggest way possible.

HAVING BEGUN MY summer back on the rez, and feeling a reconnection to my roots, I was hungry to keep my cultural awakening alive back in the city. Specifically, it became abundantly clear to me that I needed *way* more Indigenous friends in my close circle.

I still didn't really have very many Native friends. It's not like there's a convenient spot to find them in the city. How great would that be—a Home Depot–style store where you could find some Native friends? Being homesick is always going to be a factor for me as an "urban Native"—Manhattan is the polar-opposite to my home territory, after all—so I felt like having a few Native friends in the city would at least help ease the loneliness.

Lucky for me, there were two cool Native friends that I had just begun to hang out with. Claire and Inez were a couple I had met through my friend Jamie Okuma, the talented Indigenous artist. They had both just moved to New Jersey.

Claire was a Gwich'in jeweller who specialized in creating striking beaded jewellery, all made with tanned hides that she sourced, scraped, and smoked herself back home in Yellowknife. I was in awe of her work the moment I saw it on Instagram, and I wasn't the only one: her earrings and necklaces often sold out on Instagram in mere seconds. Inez, her partner, was a budding Oglala Lakota/Diné filmmaker. When we met, Inez was studying at the prestigious Tisch School of the Arts, at New York University. She had also just been hired by a major network to direct a docuseries—before she even graduated. Talk about a power couple.

To me, Claire and Inez totally symbolize Indigenous excellence: they were both excelling in fields that, historically, had not been super welcoming to our people. I found them inspiring to be around. They also were the perfect friends to talk with about Indigenous art and fashion, to kick around potential story ideas, and to broaden my knowledge of cultural traditions that aren't my own.

Plus, they were just fun as hell—we'd spend our nights laughing and laughing.

Soon enough, Claire, Inez, and I became a dynamic trio, and we would hit up the town together. Between the three of us, we knew about all the cool Native gallery openings, music performances, and fashion shows going on across the city, and we'd attend them all. Never could I have imagined that my New York social calendar would be filled to the brim with so many Indigenous events. *Every week!* It felt like the city was becoming a real hotbed for Native art and culture. I wasn't sure if this was a recent development or if Claire and Inez had just opened my eyes to what was always there. Either way, it felt like a whole new life opened up for me in the city.

It was a Friday night, and our plan was to attend a new exhibit on contemporary Native fashion at the Smithsonian Institution's National Museum of the American Indian. Located downtown in New York's financial district, the cavernous museum was hosting a cocktail party and exhibit preview, and all three of us had scored invites. Native fashion designers who had their work in the exhibit were all in town for the affair as well, and we felt it was the perfect place to network and meet some chic Native folks.

The three of us met out front at the museum and made our way inside. The lobby was already filled with tons of people—all dressed to the nines in their best Indigenous couture. Beautiful printed gowns were paired with dentalium or beaded earrings; men wore ribbon shirts along with huge turquoise rings and cowboy boots. I had worn a sleek black suit, but looking around at the outfits, I felt hugely underdressed.

We made our way upstairs to take a look around the exhibit. There were over seventy designs from more than sixty Indigenous designers. The range was impressive. There were sheer cocktail dresses adorned with elk teeth; dramatic Mylar gowns with fur trims at the bust; boots hand-beaded with imagery of swallows. These weren't the stereotypical buckskin dresses that you've seen worn in Hollywood. No, these modern, avantgarde looks showcased the best of contemporary Native style. To me, these stylish works proved that Indigenous fashion doesn't have to look a specific way; it can be incredibly diverse and forward-thinking, and not at all what you expect it to look like.

"*Yo*, look at this one," Inez said, waving me and Claire over to an adorned mannequin. It was wearing a red silk-organza gown, punctuated with a big black feather cape with embellishments of twenty-four-karat gold. It was the kind of dress you'd expect to see at the Oscars or the Met Gala—or at a couture show in Paris.

"Wow," I said, stunned by the dress.

The designer was Orlando Dugi, and he was standing just next to his dress. We introduced ourselves and began chatting.

"I *love* your work," I said, totally fangirling.

"Thank you," Orlando replied. He was wearing a perfectly tailored suit, his hair pulled back in a sleek braid. "I actually cut, sew, and dye all of the fabrics myself."

Orlando shared that, back home in Santa Fe, he often incorporated his Diné heritage into his work, and often used traditional techniques, like creating dyes made from Cochineal insects, in his designs. He wasn't just creating beautiful gala-ready pieces: he was maintaining the craftwork that his community has perfected over centuries.

A few mannequins down, we took in a big beaded parka lined entirely with fox fur. It had been made by an Inuk designer in Nunavut.

These fashions were totally blowing my mind. I had never seen such contemporary Indigenous designs before. I was used to being around the traditional side of design back home—beadwork, ribbons, quillwork—but here in New York, I was being exposed to these materials being used in exciting and unexpected new ways. I wondered why I had never heard of any of these designers before. Why wasn't anyone covering them on a major mainstream scale? To me, they all belonged in the pages of *Vogue*.

After the exhibit, Claire, Inez, and I decided to grab drinks, and some of the designers in the show joined us. *Natives night out!* We sat outside at Clandestino, a local hotspot in Dimes Square where the martinis are cheap and *good*. There, I was introduced to even more Indigenous creators: filmmakers, podcasters, designers, artists, musicians. We practically took over the bar. Every creative, in their own special way, was infusing their cultural background into their work.

Well into the night, we all cheers'd our drinks, amazed that we as Native people were able to gather in as crazy a city as New York. It did feel surreal—to see us thriving in a place that makes it so hard to follow your dreams. (They do say, "If you can make it there, you can make it anywhere.") I also couldn't believe it had taken me this long to find some Native friends in fashion. My heart felt full—like a part of it had been missing but was now back. My life in New York felt just that much more complete.

The only thing left was figuring out what the hell I was doing with it.

IT WAS NOW August; the summer was coming to a close. The city couldn't have been more hot and humid. I was in Central Park, as I always was, catching some rays while I blasted some Britney Spears on my portable speaker. I still hadn't had any luck on the job front. New York Fashion Week was coming up in September, and I was beginning to have major FOMO. I would be missing out on all the action, banished from the exclusive shows and invites and parties, now just a jobless hack.

Was I going to be a washed-up fashion writer forever?

I checked my email to see if any of my job applications had gotten a reply. Nada. *Big surprise there.* I continued to scroll and suddenly saw an email from Mandy, the friendly Australian who had for a time been my digital editor at *Footwear News*— you know, before the nightmarish editor took over and made me have a breakdown and quit.

Mandy and I had kept in touch since she'd left the magazine. She now worked for *Vogue*, where she was acting as the digital director. We would sporadically get dinner or drinks together, and we kept each other up to date on what was going on in our lives. She knew that I was currently looking for a job, so I opened up her email with a heavy dose of curiosity, and just a glimmer of hope.

"Hey Christian," she wrote. "Fashion Week is coming up in September, and *Vogue* is actually looking for a freelance producer to work here for the month. You'd be helping build the runway slideshows, and updating the site as new stories come in. Would you be interested and able to come in for an interview this week?"

I had no idea what being a digital producer meant—it sounded very technical, like I might need an IT degree for it or something. But I instantly agreed. Even though it was a temporary gig, I was elated, given it was my first job lead in months. Plus, I'd wanted to work at *Vogue* ever since I was a little kid; I grew up relishing the magazine's epic editorials, dreaming of a fantasy fashion world that had seemed so out of reach. Now, the prospect of working there was so close—in fact, it was just a job interview away. *Ah!*

Mandy and I made plans for me to come into the office and interview later that week. The magazine's headquarters, I learned, were now housed in the One World Trade Center building—a dramatic skyscraper standing tall in New York's financial district. Even though Mandy and I had a rapport, I was really nervous; I'd been told I would be meeting with *Vogue's* production manager, Melanie, during the interview. The meeting was the only thing I could think about all week.

The day of the interview, I dressed in my best suit—a sleek black number—with a fun printed shirt for a dash of personality. It's *Vogue*, after all! I checked in with the security desk, which already had me registered as a guest. The lobby felt stark and important, mostly because I knew about all of the powerful editors and writers who passed through it every day. Riding up in the elevator, I could feel my heart beating in my chest. *Dude, play it cool*, I thought. *You can't be sweating at* Vogue.

The elevator doors swooshed open to a giant lit poster that read "VOGUE." You know that angelic-choir sound effect you hear in movies or cartoons when someone reaches heaven's gates? Pretty sure I heard that exact sound at that moment. I felt like I belonged there. Mandy came out and fetched me from the lobby area. "Thank you so much for coming in," she said. "Let's head over to Melanie's office."

At the time, *Vogue* had the entire twenty-sixth floor of the building, and the rows and rows of cubicles felt polished and chic. There were tasteful portraits hanging on all of the walls—many of them taken from the black-and-white editorials that *Vogue* has published over the years, featuring the work of iconic photographers such as Irving Penn, Helmut Newton, and Annie Leibovitz. We walked by various editors and writers at their desks—all of them impeccably dressed, from what I could see without staring. Racks of designer clothes also lined some of the hallways, and as we walked by, I eyed a colourful yellow feathered coat—*Valentino?* I pondered—before we got to Melanie's office.

Melanie was *cool*. She was wearing a pair of baggy cargo pants with a fun printed mesh shirt. My nerves suddenly left the building as we chit-chatted. We talked like old friends. The whole job interview lasted about five minutes. We talked about where I had worked before, why I wanted to work at a magazine like *Vogue*, and if I was comfortable with doing more technical, behind-the-scenes work.

"Of course," I said. "Anything for *Vogue*."

She told me it would just be a one-month contract, where I'd pretty much be working five to seven days a week during Fashion Month—the industry term for the consecutive fashion weeks that are held in New York, London, Milan, and Paris during September. The producer's job was to upload all of the designer runway collections in real time as they came in, as well as to upload various writers' reviews of the collections to the website. Timeliness and precision was of key importance: *Vogue* is the authority in fashion, after all, and the entire industry comes to *Vogue* to see the collections.

I had a master plan in mind, of course. Sure, uploading photos to the website and building out stories on their online system wasn't exactly glamorous work, but it was an entry point. It was a foot in the door. Eventually, I thought, I could start pitching stories to some of the editors. Maybe even write something for the website. But I was in no big rush. Simply being in the vicinity of that glossy office, a place I'd dreamed so long of working in, was enough excitement for me. Plus, I desperately needed the cash.

"Well, I think you'd be a perfect fit," Melanie finally said. "When can you start?"

Honey, I was home.

CHAPTER 11

DEBNAMAAN GCHI GEGOO ZICHGEWIN (CATCHING A GREAT OPPORTUNITY)

IT WAS THE FIRST DAY of New York Fashion Week, and my first day of work at *Vogue*—the very magazine I had dreamed of working for since I could utter the words *Prada* and *McQueen*.

Landing at *Vogue*, even on a temporary basis, felt entirely surreal. How did a kid like me, from a small-town rez in the middle of nowhere, end up at one of the world's most prestigious fashion magazines? I couldn't believe it. I wondered over and over again how I had manifested this destiny. Sometimes I worried that I had somehow fluked into this job, and someone would eventually find me out. The feelings of imposter syndrome were *real*. Then again, fashion has a way of often making you feel inferior—like you're never chic enough, thin enough, or trendy enough.

Talk about starting out a new job with a bang, though. New

York Fashion Week was one of *Vogue*'s busiest times of the year. I would be diving headfirst into all of the fashion fun. I was also incredibly nervous. Fashion "Week" was not really a "week"; it was a month long—with the shows in London, Milan, and Paris following New York—which meant I would be working at *Vogue* for the whole month of September. I was thrilled about this. A month seemed like just enough time to network and make some connections.

I learned that I would be working with *Vogue*'s production team. The team included Melanie—the production manager who'd interviewed me for the job—and four other freelance producers like myself. We worked on a rotating schedule, and the job included many duties, but the main tasks were updating the *Vogue* homepage with all the latest fashion stories, and assisting editors or writers with building out their articles by inputting various photos and text. The most important aspect of the job, however, was uploading the runway images to the website in real time.

Since *Vogue* is the authority for the world's top designer runway collections—everyone in the industry checks *Vogue*'s website to see the new shows—timeliness and accuracy was of the utmost importance. We treated the task of uploading runway shows as seriously as a newspaper covers an election. The job required two producers on call *at all times* because we couldn't risk uploading a show even a *minute* late.

On my first day, I walked into the office trying to conceal my excitement. The magazine was housed in the Freedom Tower downtown, and the whole building had a glossy, corporate feel. It felt big—important—as if to even just walk in you needed to have a good 401K savings account and an even better credit score. And an even *better* wardrobe to match, of course. After securing my security badge, I headed up to the twenty-sixth floor, where the *Vogue* offices were located. I had gotten a sneak peek at the space when I interviewed for the job, but now I was an *employee* for the whole month; I could really poke around and get the lay of the land.

"You made it!" said Melanie as she greeted me in the stark lobby. She was, of course, in an exceptionally cool outfit again—baggy ripped jeans with a tight D&G logo shirt. I had found my people. We entered through the sleek glass doors and Melanie showed me where the production team sat. The team had a whole pod by the floor-to-ceiling windows, where I got to meet some of my fellow producers.

"Hi!" I said too enthusiastically.

I took my seat at a computer, where some of my colleagues taught me the basics of how the *Vogue* website works. I was only half listening to all the technical details; I was distracted by all of the stylish *Vogue* editors walking in and around the office, each passing ensemble more chic than the next. To my right, I spotted a mood board pinned with the faces of a variety of models, which I guessed was for an upcoming photo shoot the magazine was casting for. A fashion assistant rolled a rack of gowns past us in the hallway. It all felt like a dream—like a setting you'd see in a movie, not in real life.

When I went to use the bathroom, I looked at myself in the mirror and whispered, *"Holy shit. I'm here."*

THE PACE FOR New York Fashion Week was fast and furious.

Every day we had a busy schedule of runway shows to

upload. Some days, the production team uploaded more than twenty shows, which meant manually uploading hundreds and hundreds of images. I began to know every designer collection, and look, by heart. The metallic ruffled skirt? Rodarte! The chic cashmere sweater with the wide-leg pants? Michael Kors! It was a crash course in fashion references for that season.

Immersing myself into work at *Vogue*, I realized I was finally in the heart of the fashion industry. This was the experience I had desperately longed for. After burning out at *Footwear News* and taking some much-needed time off, I had begun to wonder if I could cut it in fashion. Was this crazy, fast-paced, cut-throat industry too much for me to handle? At one point, I had even toyed with a career change. Perhaps I should take on a well-paying corporate copywriter job and call it a day. But working at *Vogue*, my love for fashion and storytelling was re-ignited. I was finally beginning to feel a sense of purpose. It was like the Creator was tapping me on the shoulder and reminding me: *Hey, shitass, this is exactly what you're meant to be doing. You belong here.* Now I just had to prove that to the whole *Vogue* team and, hopefully, get hired once Fashion Month wrapped up.

Still, I would be lying if I said I was *totally* content. While I loved my co-workers and the producing work at *Vogue*, what I really wanted to do was write again. I didn't want to build out other writers' stories for the website; I wanted to be producing my *own* stories. I knew I had a talent for writing and finding the next best things in fashion—it was something I had done often at *Footwear News*. At *Vogue*, I just needed the chance to show what I could do, and to prove I had an eye for fashion. But I knew I had to be patient.

Working closely with the production team, I slowly got to

know all of the editors and writers at the magazine. The beauty of being tasked with uploading all of their stories to the website was that we were in frequent communication. Sometimes, editors and writers would come over to the production section to ask us questions in person, and I wanted to use this to my advantage. I knew I had to get to know the whole team if I ever wanted to pitch stories and write for the magazine. It became a game for me—finding opportunities to chit-chat with various staff members wherever I could. "Do you know where so-and-so sits," I'd ask an editor who was sitting at their desk, even though I already knew damn well where so-and-so sat.

The *Vogue* staff was as cool and fashionable as you'd imagine them to be. Each writer seemed to offer a unique point of view to the team—not to mention each had their own individual personal style. Some dressed edgy-cool, and had a vast knowledge of all the up-and-coming designers. Others dressed timeless and chic, and had a keen eye for the trends of the season. But, even better, everyone was extremely kind and normal—not at all like the stuffy, stuck-up fashionistas who are so often portrayed in TV or film.

One editor I immediately clicked with was Jennie, *Vogue*'s digital fashion news editor at the time. Jennie spearheaded all of the fashion content for the website, and she was just damn *cool*. Originally from South Korea, she had an impressive knowledge of all the emerging, avant-garde designers coming out of the country. (She also had a special focus on and interest in K-pop stars.) Her whole look was very avant-garde: she had bright red hair, wore towering Balenciaga or Rick Owens platforms every day, and her outfits were edgy and sleek. She was a bit of a caricature of a cool fashion person—and I loved that.

I knew I wanted to write for her. No, I *had* to write for her.

Once New York Fashion Week began winding down, I asked Jennie if she would like to grab lunch with me upstairs in the Condé Nast cafeteria. I wanted to pick her brain on some story ideas, and to see if she would be interested in having me write for her.

The Condé cafeteria was a real New York media scene. And lunch time was prime time. It's where you could spot writers and editors from magazines like *GQ*, the *New Yorker*, *Vogue*, *Vanity Fair*, and more, all mingling and gossiping about work over sandwiches and salads.

Jennie accepted my invitation and we headed up to the thirty-fifth floor and took a table next to the floor-to-ceiling windows, which offered a striking view of the Hudson River, and even the Statue of Liberty in the distance. It was such a scenic view, it almost looked fake.

"So, how was your Fashion Week," I asked as we dug into our salads.

"It was cool—there were a lot of new, young designers that I really loved seeing," Jennie said. "You guys must have been busy on the production team!"

"Yeah, it was kind of crazy," I said, mid-bite. "But I loved that I got to see all of the shows while uploading them. I feel like I was there."

I asked her about where she was from, how long she had been at *Vogue*, and what kind of stories she was looking for from writers. Of course, I already had one in mind.

"I actually have a story idea I wanted to run by you—and feel free to say no," I continued.

"Oh, let's hear it!" she said.

I had been crafting the idea in my head since my very first week at *Vogue*. I wanted to bring a more personal perspective to the magazine; particularly, I wanted to write about Indigenous fashion, something I felt was still very much a niche. I knew my culture had beautiful design traditions—it's something I grew up seeing at our summer powwows or community events—and I knew of so many contemporary Native designers who were creating beautiful, fashion-forward works as well. To me, they all seemed *Vogue*-worthy. I wanted to write a story that would highlight them all.

"I'm Indigenous," I continued, "and I'd love to pitch a package spotlighting Native designers. What I love about them is they're all infusing their heritage and traditions into their designs. It's a way of reclaiming their history. And it's not something that's been covered a lot."

I could tell by Jennie's face that she had never been pitched such a story before.

"Oh, interesting," she said after a quick ponder. "You're right, I don't think we've written much about Native designers. Do you have any photos of their work?"

Later that day, I created a deck of images for Jennie to review. I decided on six Native designers who already had large followings for their work, and compiled photos of their latest designs. I picked the best of the best.

On the list were talents like the Luiseño/Shoshone-Bannock designer Jamie Okuma, whose intricate beadwork was already on display in museums like the Met, and experimental designers like Lil'wat artist Curtis Oland, who made use of raw, natural fabrics. There was the Kiowa jeweller Keri Ataumbi, based in Santa Fe, who worked in silver, gold, and precious stones. I wanted to offer a diverse mix of artists who could showcase the breadth and variety of Native design, to show that Native fashion doesn't look one way. To show that we are not all the same.

"I would love for you to write this," Jennie finally replied to my email, after I waited on pins and needles for hours. I was thrilled. I had just gotten my first writing assignment for *Vogue*!

She added that *Vogue* would be taking my story on-spec— meaning, there was no guarantee they would publish it or pay me for it until I handed in the final draft. This was standard for new writers, and a risky assignment, but it was a risk I was willing to take. I knew I had to prove myself. Once they read about these designers and saw their beautiful work, I was confident the piece would be a go. I wasn't worried. Game on.

OVER THE NEXT two weeks, I focused all my time on crafting my very first piece for *Vogue*.

By day, I was still working on the production team, uploading designer collections from London, Milan, and Paris to *Vogue*'s website. But by night, or on the weekends during my free time, I was busy interviewing the six Native designers, and learning about how their respective nations influenced their work.

Jeweller Keri Ataumbi told me about how she often combined her culture's traditional materials (quills, feathers) with high-tech goldsmithing or 3-D printing techniques; Evan Ducharme, a Métis designer in Vancouver, shared how his family lineage comes through in his designs; for example, he found a census form filled out by his great-grandfather, and then screen-printed it onto his bomber jackets, skirts, and bags.

While the works of the six Native designers couldn't have

been more different on paper, I was struck by a through-line that encompassed all their collections. Each was using fashion as a means to celebrate and elevate their cultural traditions. To them, fashion design was less about the aesthetic and more about the storytelling behind it. I loved this idea. To me, that's what constitutes the best fashion—a story that goes deeper than just the design.

A few weeks later, the piece was done, and I sent it over to Jennie. I had butterflies in my stomach. I had spent many nights writing and rewriting it. To me, it was the most important story that I had *ever written* in my career to date, and I treated it as such. This was my chance to not only impress *Vogue* but, more importantly, to introduce Indigenous fashion to a whole new audience.

No pressure.

A day or two later, Jennie wrote back. "This is amazing," she said. "I just made a few small changes. Have a look and let me know what you think . . . Can we run it this week?"

Since I was already on *Vogue*'s production team, I even had the lucky task of uploading and building out my own story for the website. I chose each designer's very best looks, wanting the imagery to pop off the page and really showcase just how awesome Indigenous design is. Seeing the piece all built and ready on *Vogue*'s website, I had a moment of disbelief—not only because I was seeing my byline on the website, but also because I was seeing Indigenous fashion spotlighted in such a big way.

When we published the story, I was immediately excited to share the article on all of my social platforms: Facebook, Instagram, Twitter—I did a major *blast*. I was so proud of it! After years of failing to connect with my work, I'd finally written a story that felt both personal and monumental.

A few days went by, and the piece began to circulate online and pick up traffic among Indian Country (it's what us Native folks call our community). It didn't take long for other Native fashion creatives to take notice—mostly because such a major publication had never featured them or their friends before. The feedback was almost instantaneous.

"Never thought I would see the day Indigenous fashion is in *Vogue*!"

"WE'RE IN *VOGUE*??"

"More of these types of stories, *Vogue*!"

Across social media, all sorts of Indigenous designers, artists, models, and more were sharing their support for my story. Like me, they too had felt ignored—and marginalized—by the mainstream fashion industry. So much so that a mainstream magazine like *Vogue* highlighting their culture felt entirely surreal. It still felt that way to me, too.

By no means am I tooting my own horn here, but it was at that moment when I realized my work could have a bigger impact than just spotlighting the latest collections and trends. It was clear that Indigenous people needed to be seen and heard in fashion, and that my writing could help amplify their voices. For many people, having their culture amplified is deeply meaningful. It seemed, to me, the perfect opportunity—to use a platform like *Vogue* to spotlight underrepresented cultures.

The piece went on to become one of *Vogue*'s best-performing stories of the month. I had known for a while that there was a big appetite for Indigenous fashion, both from Indigenous and non-Indigenous folks. And with this first piece, I now had the receipts—concrete proof!—which meant I could continue to pitch such stories moving forward.

Little did I know this was just the beginning.

BEFORE I KNEW it, my Fashion Month at *Vogue* came to an end. I was proud of navigating such a busy time and, more importantly, for getting a byline out of it before my last day.

I had hoped to miraculously be hired full-time by the magazine at the end of the month—but sadly, my contract came to a close, and there were no job openings as of yet. My dream of working at *Vogue* would have to wait.

Even so, I regularly kept up with the team as I went back to my freelance life. And luckily, my work with *Vogue* didn't *totally* end. I was generously offered a part-time contract, where I was asked to write for *Vogue*'s digital site about three days a week. This felt totally glamorous to me—being able to pop in and out of the magazine, occasionally writing about red carpets and trends and celebrity style. The work was fun, too—exactly the type of content that I wanted to write about.

Some days, I would go into the office to work, or I'd just come in for meetings on an as-needed basis. I was starting to feel like part of the family, someone the whole team knew and depended on. I received many compliments from staff about my Indigenous fashion piece. The article certainly got me noticed. Like all of the other impossibly cool *Vogue* writers and editors who have a niche, I had something that differentiated me from all the other fashion writers in the city. I realized that my knowledge of Indigenous fashion was now my "It factor."

One day, I had just come back to my desk from lunch when I

got an email from Courtney, *Vogue*'s executive editor. "Do you have two seconds to chat?" she asked.

Was I in trouble?

I walked over to her corner office and sat down.

"Hi!"

"So, we actually have a full-time position opening up that I wanted to run by you," she said.

My ears perked up.

"Elliott, our long-time style editor, is leaving us," she said. "We're looking for someone who can join our team full-time to write about fashion. This would include trends, red carpets, celebrity style, designer profiles. You've been producing a lot of great content over the past few weeks, and we thought you would be a natural fit."

I tried to play it cool. Was I about to get hired at *Vogue*?

"I would love that," I said, giving my best poker face. "That sounds like a dream."

"You would have to be interviewed by Anna, of course," said Courtney.

My excitement immediately turned into butterflies.

Anna Wintour was the long-standing editor of *Vogue*, and a bona fide icon. It's no secret that the entire fashion industry practically revolves around her. Designers give her exclusive first looks at their collections, and she supports the next generation of designers, too, through programs like the CFDA/ *Vogue* Fashion Fund. She knows industry news before anybody else and can predict where fashion is headed before anyone else. And she is also, notably, the driving force behind the star-studded Met Gala—the museum's biggest fundraising and charity event of the year.

And now, I would be interviewing with her for a job.

I felt like throwing up.

It was near the end of the year, and December arrived quickly. Winter in New York was one of my favourite times of the year. Sure, some people complain about the cold and the snow, but I loved when the various storefronts became all festive with their fake snow and twinkling lights and cheap Santa Claus decorations. To me, it was a magical time. I still hadn't heard about when my job interview with Anna would occur, but as work was beginning to slow down for the holiday season, I found myself checking my inbox obsessively—convinced that I'd somehow missed the email, or that it had gone to my spam folder. Nothing yet.

I did have a travel opportunity to distract myself with, though. It was from *Vogue*'s living editor, Ellen, who oversaw all of the website's food, travel, and wedding content. "Do you want to travel to Germany to tour its Christmas markets? They're world-famous," she wrote to me in an email. All I read were the words *free trip* and *writing job*.

"Yes!" I replied, way too quickly.

In the beginning of December, I spent just over a week touring Germany's vast Christmas markets—a totally impromptu jaunt. Rather than visiting the cool big cities like Berlin or Munich, I spent a week zigzagging through spots like Erfurt, Weimar, and Thuringia, all of which were famous for their festive holiday markets.

Though I had a point of contact in each of these small cities, I was largely left to my own devices—and the locals, to my surprise, barely spoke English. I dulled my loneliness by partaking in lots of pretzels, bratwurst, and mulled wine. *So* much mulled wine. I have a pounding headache just thinking about the night I overdid it.

I was staying in Weimar at the Hotel Elephant—a very Wes Anderson–esque hotel where, creepily enough, Hitler used to love to stay—when I got the email on my phone.

"Can you meet with Anna on Friday?"

I had almost totally forgotten about the job interview. Not really—but it had taken so long to materialize that I had begun to think it wasn't going to happen. I froze in panic. Seeing how I was currently in the middle of nowhere in a foreign German city, how in the hell was I going to get to an interview with Anna? I double-checked my trip's itinerary. Turns out, I was flying back on Thursday. I *could* make back in time.

"Yes, of course," I replied swiftly.

I could only half focus on the remainder of the trip as I headed onwards to Thuringia. Touring one of its most famous landmarks, the Wartburg castle, I was in awe of its location, perched thirteen hundred feet up in the mountains, overlooking the countryside. But while I was touring the grounds, I could focus on only one thing: What I would wear for my Anna interview? While fellow tourists took a seat beside me on a bench, speaking of the splendours of the castle and its history, I was already busy inputting "Prada" and "Dior" into eBay or TheRealReal.

What does one wear for a job interview with Anna Wintour?

THE DAY BEFORE my interview, I landed in New York, with only a few hours available to find an outfit. I felt pressure to deliver that perfectly stylish job interview look. This was *Vogue*! Sure, my qualifications and personality were the most important thing, but it's no secret that securing a position at a fashion magazine is about your personal style, too. You have to bring your own unique flair and eye to the role, after all. You wouldn't hire a personal decorator with horrible furniture taste, would you? In fashion, the clothes a person wears tell you everything about them. I wanted to make a statement, and to showcase my point of view through style.

My friend Dianne kindly agreed to meet me at Barneys (R.I.P), a ritzy uptown department store known for the legendary list of designers that it carried. Prada, Dries Van Noten, Balmain, Rick Owens—it had it all. I needed a friend to shop with, someone who could give me an honest second opinion. My future at *Vogue* depended on this outfit! Luckily, Barneys was having a big blowout sale—meaning, hopefully, I could find an outfit for cheap(ish).

Only problem was, I was beginning to feel deathly ill.

During my last few days in Germany, I had caught some sort of weird travel flu. My nose would not stop leaking, and I was now graced with a bona fide smoker's cough. I was losing my voice. I felt like I was malfunctioning, or like my body was shutting down. But I powered through anyway and headed to Barneys, fresh off my flight, determined to find the perfect outfit. Postponing or cancelling the job interview was simply not an option. I would crawl there on my hands and knees, or hooked up to an IV, if need be.

I rolled up to Barneys, my gigantic suitcase in tow. I hacked up a lung as I paid my taxi fare. Dianne was already there waiting.

"You ready?" she said, helping me wheel my huge suitcase into the store.

"Let's do this," I said in my hoarse voice.

Given the blowout sale, the store was in total chaos. Tourists and locals alike were rushing through the racks of designer clothes, which were going for more than 50 to 80 percent off. We could barely wheel my suitcase through the madness. It was a zoo.

We took the escalator up to the menswear floor.

"So, what should we look for?" Dianne said as we glided up slowly.

"Well, I'll probably wear one of my suits, but I want some sort of fun top to go with it," I said. "Something fun, but still professional."

"Roger that," she said as we hopped off on the upper floor.

We started to peruse the men's sale racks together. The sale was *good*—there's a reason that Barneys sales were legendary (and likely why it went out of business). Designer runway pieces were going for as cheap as $100. I was optimistic I'd find something.

We got to the Prada section, and my eyes lit up. Discreetly tucked in to one of the racks was a colourful button-up shirt that was 80 percent off. It was printed with rows and rows of cartoony lipsticks—a signature print of the label. I was shocked that such an iconic piece was going for just $250. I wondered if the markdown was a mistake; it's a shirt that usually costs around $2,000. I immediately headed to the change room to try it on.

"Christian, let's see," Dianne called out impatiently from outside the dressing room.

To my surprise, the shirt fit perfectly. I came out and did a little twirl for Dianne. "You have to get it," she said. "It's so good." I had to agree. It was the perfect top to wear with my black suit, offering just a dash of print and fun to the otherwise sleek look.

Mission accomplished!

I had another coughing fit as I headed to the register. The snooty sales associate looked at me like I had the plague (and honestly, I probably did). My sickness seemed to be getting worse—not better—but I ignored it, thinking only of the fashion look I knew I had to slay while walking into Anna's office the next day.

IT WAS THE morning of my big job interview, and I was dressed in my sleekest black suit and my new Prada shirt. I had to admit, I looked like a *Vogue* writer. The outfit was the perfect balance of trendy and timeless. I added some heeled black boots for a little more flair.

I looked chic.

I took the express train downtown to the Freedom Tower, *Vogue*'s headquarters. The train seemed to be travelling at light speed, causing me to frequently lose my balance in my heeled boots. On the subway, I stood across from someone reading the latest issue of *Vogue*—it felt like a good omen, a cheeky sign from the Creator telling me, *You've got this.*

I certainly hoped I did.

I arrived a good thirty minutes early to the tall skyscraper, leaving no chance of being late. One is not late for a *Vogue* job interview with Anna Wintour. After killing some time outside, I made my way into the building. My freelance pass still worked, so I was told by Anna's assistants that they would meet me upstairs in the twenty-sixth floor lobby.

I was incredibly nervous, but I had been working at *Vogue* for some time now, so there was a level of comfort and familiarity when I stepped off the elevator. While I had never met Anna one-on-one before, we had been in some of the same staff meetings, and she was aware of my work. Still, the idea of walking into her office would make anyone nervous. She was someone I'd respected and admired since I was a little tweenager, after all. I had no choice—I had to make a good impression.

One of Anna's assistants fetched me from the lobby at 11 a.m., right on the dot. "She's ready to see you now," she said, warmly welcoming me through the big glass doors.

Gulp.

To get to Anna's office, you have to walk past her two assistants, who sit perched at desks on either side of her office. I waved hello to her second assistant as I glided in, trying to look cool, confident, and not at all like I was about to have an anxiety attack.

Anna's office was large and flanked by floor-to-ceiling windows that made the space feel bright and airy. There were elegant flowers, paintings, and vases everywhere—a stylish space that could easily have its own tour on *Architectural Digest*. Anna was sitting at her desk when I walked in, and I greeted her with a firm handshake. "Nice to meet you," I said calmly. I wondered if she had ever had someone Indigenous, let alone from a rez, in her office before; once again, my imposter syndrome was beginning to shine through.

"Please, have a seat," she said, as I tried to shimmy into one of the metal chairs.

We chatted about where I had worked before, and how long I had been working at *Vogue*. She clearly was already familiar with my writing—it was more about getting to know each other. We talked about what books I was reading at the moment, and if there were any Broadway plays I had enjoyed recently. To my surprise, she asked me very little about fashion; I got the sense that she wanted to gauge if I had interests in fields outside of style.

The meeting lasted just over five minutes, and she thanked me for coming in. Talk about short and sweet.

All things considered, I thought I had done the best I could. During our interview, she was warm, professional, and seemed interested in my background—which is all I could have hoped for. Still, it was hard to guess whether I had impressed her or not. It's hard to dazzle someone in just under five minutes. But maybe that was Anna's grand test, to see if I could somehow be memorable in three hundred seconds.

At least she totally eyed my new Prada shirt.

CHAPTER 12

GCHI-NENDMOWIN
(EXCITEMENT)

I GOT THE CALL OUT of the blue.

A few torturous weeks had passed since I had my big interview with Anna at *Vogue*, and I was beginning to think that I hadn't landed the gig. Oh well. I had come to peace with it. At least it was a good experience. I was honoured to even be considered. The opportunity would be a memorable story for my memoir one day. (Wink, wink.)

But then an HR representative from Condé Nast called me and told me that I got the job. I asked her to repeat herself—I was unsure that I had heard her correctly.

"Your title would be *Vogue*'s fashion and style writer," she said, as I tried not to scream with glee into the phone. "How does that sound?"

I thought the title sounded fancy—if not a little superfluous. Fashion *and* style writer? Are they not the same thing? Whatever. It all sounded so glamorous. Besides, you could basically call me *Vogue*'s anything and I would be happy with the title. It was the magazine that I had dreamed of working at since I was a little kid.

My dream had come true.

I was told that I would be reporting on celebrity red carpets, analyzing fashion trends, doing designer profiles, and basically writing about anything else that interested me. I got the sense from our phone call that, to work at *Vogue*, each writer needed a distinct "thing"—something that would set them apart from the pack, and something that would give them—and their work—an inimitable "cool factor."

I saw huge potential here. I knew I wanted to write more about my Indigenous culture and, specifically, all of the cool things that were happening within the Indigenous fashion space. Plus, being able to write about those things on a platform like *Vogue*, which has such a huge international audience, provided a powerful opportunity—to introduce readers to a whole new vibrant (and underrepresented) community. So many people still think of Indigenous folks as relics of the past, and not a community that is still here. Fashion, I thought, could be a medium through which to change that.

"That sounds amazing," I said coolly. "When do I start?"

FOR MY FIRST few months on the job, I really tried to play the part of a *Vogue* writer—I wore the high-fashion designer clothes that you'd assume someone at a fashion magazine wears.

Though I had freelanced for *Vogue* for a while now, I was still extremely intimidated by the whole work environment. Everyone at *Vogue* dressed so *cool*. And put together. And posh. And, somehow, effortless. So I, too, tried to cosplay as an impossibly chic writer. If my life were a movie, this would be the part where an epic fashion montage happens.

Cue Madonna's "Vogue"! Picture me walking into the office wearing the craziest outfits you can think of—whether a full-on Canadian tuxedo or a sequin shirt with metallic shoes (worn at, like, noon on a Tuesday). Every day, I came dressed to impress, even if my outfits were (often) a miss.

I began working closely with my boss, Chioma, *Vogue*'s fashion director, who was a fabulous Brit with a distinctive accent and the coolest wardrobe I'd ever seen (even to this day!). Every morning, Chioma would saunter into the office wearing graphic Jean Paul Gaultier mesh skirts and tops, or the latest cool Balenciaga bag. I admired her fashion eye—she knew of every cool designer before anyone else did—and she was an even better editor, making my own work continuously stronger and better with her feedback. If a piece I handed in wasn't good, she'd let me know. I loved her honesty.

Our fashion team consisted of me, Chioma, fashion news editor Jennie—who'd given me my first big *Vogue* byline!—and three other writers named Lisa, Janae, and Renée. I was intimidated by all of them, even if they were my colleagues. Each of the writers had their own distinct vibe and fashion sense going on. Lisa was a quirky writer whose brain served as an encyclopedia of anything '90s or 2000s fashion related; Janae interviewed all of the A-list celebrities and had an impressive knowledge of every working model on the scene;

and Renée had more of a cool Brooklyn-girl vibe to her—she DJ'd on the weekends, and often covered up-and-coming musicians, too.

And then there was me. The new guy.

I quickly realized that I, too, needed a "thing." If I wanted to hang out with the cool kids, I, too, would need some sort of cool factor. Sure, I had gotten the job already, but if I wanted to stand out and be a real *Vogue* writer, I needed to carve out a niche for myself.

So, I began pitching stories that reflected my interests.

The fashion team had its weekly pitch meeting coming up, and I wanted to bring some fresh story ideas to the table. Sitting at my new desk, I thought long and hard about what to pitch. Generally, I knew I wanted to write about Indigenous designers and artists who were channelling their culture into their work—something that I felt was rarely covered by mainstream fashion magazines at the time (and still today).

I wish I could say that this mission statement came from some high-and-mighty place of wanting to increase Indigenous representation in fashion—and on some level, it certainly did—but frankly, my interest came from a more selfish place: I was simply *in love* with so many Indigenous designers on the scene, and I just wanted the chance to talk to them and get inside their creative minds. There was now a professional reason for me to fangirl.

While my first Indigenous fashion piece had performed well, I knew I wanted to follow it up with even more and better stories. So, brainstorming ideas at my desk, I tried to think about another aspect of the Indigenous fashion world that would appeal to a wider *Vogue* readership. I wanted to write about something beautiful (obviously), but also something that would have impact and meaning.

Think, Christian. Think.

Oh, *duh!*

Beadwork!

Growing up on the rez, I was consistently surrounded by beadwork. My earliest childhood memories involved seeing my aunties making beaded moccasins, or other beaded pieces and jewellery for powwow regalia. I have always loved the beautiful colours of beads, and how neatly and tightly they're arranged onto a garment or earring. It's so satisfying to look at—and even more satisfying to see beadworkers in action making them. It's a skill that requires a lot of time, patience, and love. Talk about the best example of *slow fashion*: some beaded pieces take weeks, if not months, to complete. A lot of intention goes into a single piece.

So, what if I did a *Vogue* piece highlighting different Indigenous beadwork artists?

I had been obsessively following various Indigenous beadwork artists on Instagram. When I say obsessively, I mean *obsessively*. I would spend hours and hours scrolling through various Instagram pages, saving posts and accounts that featured work ranging from earrings to medallions to moccasins to bags. The world of Indigenous beadwork, it seemed, was exploding with creativity and innovation, and I wanted to write about it. After all, there were so many different styles and techniques of beadwork out there—there was *so much* material to work with! By showcasing a few of these artists, I also wanted to showcase how Native beadwork doesn't have to look one specific way, and nor should it. It can be anything from pretty floral earrings to an edgy beaded bag with studs, spikes, and skulls.

I pitched the story idea to Chioma and Jennie, who, thankfully, were immediately into it.

"Wow, these are *beautiful*," Chioma said as I showed her some photos of beadwork on my iPhone. "I'd love to hear more about where they're from, and what inspires their pieces."

I landed on profiling eight different beadworkers. On the roster were talents like Crow artist Elias Jade Not Afraid, who has a unique approach to doing beaded florals and skulls; Dene artist Skye Paul, who gives beadwork a fun, cartoonish pop art treatment; and Molina Two Bulls, who is Oglala Lakota and Northern Cheyenne and specializes in cool, graphic cuffs. The work of each of these artists was visually stunning, yes, but they all had different stories and backgrounds that showcased the variety of Indigenous communities, too.

When I reached out to interview the various artists, almost all of them had the exact same response.

"I *never* thought I would be in *Vogue*!"

"I thought this email was a scam! I couldn't believe it was real!"

This, to me, was the best part of my new job. Not only did I get to write about cool people doing cool things, but I got to amplify their work. For so many underrepresented designers, getting spotlighted in *Vogue* was an unbelievable, career-defining moment. It was a *major* stamp of approval. To me, their work and craftsmanship and attention to detail rivals any European couture house.

I spent weeks putting the story together, from the

interviewing process to the writing process. Finally, I was happy with the piece, and I submitted my second Indigenous-focused *Vogue* story. When the beadwork article was posted online a little while later, it became one of *Vogue*'s most popular stories of the week. Again.

I knew I had struck gold with this type of fashion storytelling. It was clear that readers wanted this kind of content. Why? The works that Indigenous artists create are not just visually stunning; the backstory and context of their pieces capture people's attention too. I was so pleased that these stories were resonating with an audience that, for the most part, was unfamiliar with Indigenous culture and practices.

A few days after the story went live, I received a nice note from my boss, Chioma: "This is exactly the type of story I want you to keep doing," she said. "Nice work!"

My Indigenous fashion coverage was here to stay.

I had finally found my cool factor.

ALTHOUGH I WAS beginning to carve out my own space at *Vogue*, I would be lying if I said it wasn't a lonely experience at times. On one hand, the whole fashion team was supportive of my ideas: they encouraged me to find all types of Indigenous stories to tell. This was a stark difference to the beginning of my career, when I would pitch Indigenous-focused ideas to other publications and not even receive a response.

But, on the other hand, there were no Indigenous folks at *Vogue* who I could also bounce ideas around with. I certainly felt a duty to represent Native people as a whole, especially as one of the only Native people on staff. But like in any environment where you are a minority, the experience could be isolating at times—in the sense that there was added pressure for me not only to tell these stories (who else would?) but to tell the *right* Indigenous stories, and to profile the *right* artists.

Problem was, I was no *expert* in Indigenous fashion and culture. I was learning just as much as my readers were. But I had a drive and a passion to learn more, so I continued pitching stories and writing articles with a heavy dose of curiosity and interest. And, in the process, I slowly *did* become an expert of sorts—familiarizing myself with all kinds of design traditions and customs, whether Kiowa, Cree, Navajo, or others.

Outside of work, my Indigenous besties in the city—Claire and Inez—were perfect sounding boards for brainstorming new *Vogue* story ideas. Over drinks at our favourite haunts, we would discuss the possibilities. Perhaps I should write about a new show coming out with an Indigenous cast, or a new Native model we had discovered. Those happy-hour discussions were invaluable to me and my writing process. (And, like my editor Chioma, Claire and Inez would also tell me if an idea was shit.)

"Dude, you're totally doing important work at *Vogue*," Inez said to me as we ordered a second round of gin and tonics at Barcade—a New York chain of bars where you can play pinball machines and retro arcade games. We were about to play Pac-Man.

"You think?" I said, unsure of such praise.

"Yes! It's an opportunity for a total revolution," said Claire, who always spoke with an intensity that I loved. "Our people would not be written about in mainstream fashion spaces without you. You're totally paving the way."

At the time, I rolled my eyes, thinking she was gassing me up like any good friend would. But later that night, as I got back home to my tiny studio in the Upper East Side, I took in her statement. In a way, it was true: Would Indigenous designers *ever* be in *Vogue* if a Native person didn't step up and pitch these stories? It was a long overdue moment. This realization came with a sense of weight and responsibility—and sometimes with anxiety attacks. It felt like a lot of pressure for one person to handle.

But luckily, thanks to community, I didn't have to do it totally alone.

WHEN I WASN'T busy strategizing my Indigenous takeover at *Vogue*, I was busy fulfilling my other daily job duties, one of which was interviewing celebrities for the magazine.

As a fashion writer, one of my main duties was reporting on celebrity fashion—whether it was what the stars were wearing out on the streets or on the red carpets during awards season. This often led to interviews with celebrities, too. After all, many of them had their own fashion brands to promote, or they would want to talk about the inspiration behind a look that they were wearing for a big, splashy movie premiere. There was *always* an A-lister available for a ten-minute chat.

This all felt so fun and exciting to me. Not only did I get one-on-one time with some of my favourite performers, but I got to chat about all things *fashion* with them. Basically, this meant that I was writing about my two childhood obsessions—fashion and Hollywood—in a job where I was now being *paid* to obsess over those same things.

Could someone pinch me?

It wasn't lost on me how cool my job was. Some days, I would hop on the phone with a pop superstar to discuss the fashion direction in her new music video. Other days, I'd head to a fashion event and spend five minutes chit-chatting with a hot new TV star. Or I'd meet up for coffee with a supermodel to discuss a fashion designer she was about to walk for. I simply didn't know what each week held in store, and I loved the spontaneity.

Vogue had unparalleled access to celebrities—nobody ever said no to *Vogue*—on a level that I had never quite experienced before. At previous jobs, I'd gotten used to begging for any sort of good celebrity interviews; now, the star-studded opportunities were coming in fast and furious—and even better yet, they were all mine for the taking.

As a result, I quickly got *very good* at interviewing celebrities. To me, it really is a skill and an art form. You not only want to connect and engage with your subject, but you also have to do it in a very short amount of time. Ruthless Hollywood publicists are known to cut you off after a brief five to ten minutes—fifteen minutes, if you're lucky. Thankfully, I was never one for mindless small talk: I loved diving right into our chats, like an assassin.

But why did I *really* feel like I was good at celebrity interviews? Because I treated them like, well, *humans.* I did so many celebrity interviews a day that I quickly stopped getting starstruck. Skipping over the fawning or fangirling, I'd casually chat with A-listers like they were an old friend. I'd let the conversation go where it wanted to go, never once trying to get "the soundbite" or posing the gotcha-style questions that so many other celebrity reporters ask. I'd like to believe that all of the stars I've chatted with could sense that.

In one particular instance, for example, I was set to interview a certain iconic character actress who was starring in a buzzy new vacation-themed show. The publicist had set aside twenty minutes for us to chat over the phone; instead, we ended up chatting for a staggering *two and a half hours*—covering a wide range of topics ranging from what her acting process is to why she believed her house might or might not be haunted.

"*No, please stay on,*" she said, after I considerately tried to wrap up the convo at the twenty-minute mark. "*I'm having fun!* I love your questions."

I'm not sharing this to brag or to pretend like I'm best friends with celebrities. (Spoiler alert: I'm not.) At the end of the day, we're all just doing a job. But I *did* feel like I was connecting with my work, and, frankly, I was realizing one thing: I was good at it.

SEPTEMBER ROLLED AROUND, and New York Fashion Week was kicking off in the city. This would be my first Fashion Month as a full-time *Vogue* writer, and I was excited about all of the possibilities. For one, I had never gotten seats at any *good* runway shows (Rodarte, Marc Jacobs, Proenza Schouler), but now I would maybe, *maybe*, be getting a good ticket or two. I also knew that I would be getting some amazing celebrity interview pitches: publicists had already begun flooding me with a bevy of opportunities.

"My client is going to so-and-so's show. Do you want to interview them backstage?"

"Do you want to do a getting-ready diary with her? And cover her amazing looks?"

"PLEASE—What can I do to get her in *Vogue*??"

About midway through Fashion Week, though, the best celebrity interview opportunity came my way.

"Do you have a second?" Chioma asked as I stepped into her office.

"The Ralph Lauren show is tomorrow," she continued, "and [an A-list, Oscar-winning actress] is attending. Would you want to go to the show and interview her backstage?"

I laughed. "Who would ever say no to that?"

I mentioned a few paragraphs back that I rarely get starstruck—but in the case of this particular actress, I was incredibly nervous. I *loved* her work and had watched almost everything she'd been in up to that point. Still, I put my professional hat on and, back at my desk, started coming up with some questions that I thought were thoughtful, fun, and stylish.

Attending the Ralph Lauren show—one of New York's biggest and most lavish productions—was a real treat. That season, the iconic American designer was staging his show inside an old Wall Street bank down in the Financial District. Ralph transformed the space into "Ralph's Club," an art deco–style lounge (just for the night) complete with a live jazz band. All of the guests, myself included, were dressed in formal tuxedos and evening gowns. Martinis were being passed around like water. There were chic little bowls of mixed nuts everywhere, and these cute little bistro tables with cute little table lamps on them. It all felt like a scene out of a movie or something— totally surreal and, of course, extremely glamorous. I was obsessed.

A publicist found me as I was entering the event space. She told me that I would be interviewing the Oscar-winning actress shortly before the show began.

"It's very loud in here!" she said above the sound of the band, "so we'll find a quiet space for the two of you to chat."

I was nervous but excited. The problem with doing a fashion show in a defunct bank space? Turns out, there are few quiet corners to conduct an interview in. The publicist found me a few minutes later. "We'll have you two chat in this closet," she said.

She guided me towards a tiny, cramped, dark janitor's closet that had two dusty chairs in it—as well as an old bucket of paint on the side. It was a stark contrast to the elevated decor just a few feet outside. Here I was, about to be chatting with a top Hollywood star, talking about fashion for *Vogue*, in a decrepit closet, as though we were playing a high-school game of Seven Minutes in Heaven or something.

I chuckled as she arrived, looking as fabulous as ever.

"*Ah, the glamour,*" the star joked as she entered the claustrophobic closet.

The show that followed the interview was very luxurious and elegant. Supermodels such as Bella Hadid slinked out in Ralph's signature evening gowns and tuxedo suits. I sipped on a martini as I took in the crowd, which was extremely star-studded. It was a classic New York night—the type of night that reminds you why New York is the best, and worth dealing with all of the rats, garbage, and street pee. Why? Because, sometimes, there's also fashion, celebrities, good clothes, and even better cocktails.

I had one of the best seats in the house for the show, perched on a level just above the main crowd, giving me a bird's-eye view of everything going on. At the end, singer Janelle Monáe even came out to do a medley of jazz-style songs, totally bringing down the house with her energetic and theatrical performance. I had to pinch myself as the show ended. My life felt so *cool and exciting.* For the first time in my career, I was beginning to feel like I had truly made it. And even better, I felt like I deserved to be there.

And then the world came to a big, screeching halt.

IN MARCH OF 2020, a pandemic changed life as we knew it.

A deadly virus known as COVID-19 ripped through our communities, threatened everything we knew, and, in some cases, took the ones we loved the most.

I was on my way to work when I got the email from our digital director. News reports of the growing COVID-19 pandemic had already begun making headlines around the world, but until that point, we had been operating normally—totally oblivious and naively unaware of what was truly coming our way. The email changed all of that. "Please stay home, and we will be working from home indefinitely," it read.

A few days later, panic took over the whole city. New Yorkers, myself included, were now scared to even step outside, terrified that we'd catch this mysterious and deadly plague.

I had worked so hard to get to *Vogue*, and now that every-thing was falling into place, all of that was in jeopardy. I know there were way bigger worries to think about—like, you know, not dying. But frankly, one of my main anxieties at the time was that all my hopes and dreams were about to be ripped away from me. Yes, I was scared. But even more vividly, I remember being angry. Annoyed. *Pissed.*

My parents urged me to come back home to Canada. They did not feel safe having me in New York all by myself, espe-cially as the pandemic seemed to be worsening. So, I made the (probably not safe) decision to book a flight home to Nipissing so that I could be close to family. When I boarded the flight, barely anyone was wearing a mask.

Was this whole pandemic thing an exaggeration?

A few days later, the international borders were closed. I had made it out just in time.

Over the next year, I mostly stayed cooped up at my parents' house. Living out in the country, where I could go days with-out seeing another human being, felt both safe—*could I catch COVID if I never interacted with anyone?*—and isolating.

A depression quickly creeped into my bones, though I was hardly alone in that general feeling of despair. Every night, I would fix myself several martinis to cope with it all, picking up that bad drinking habit yet again. I gained a *lot* of weight, and began to care less and less about what I looked like. I lost my sense of identity, purpose, *and* my sense of style. (But admit it, you wore only sweatpants for most of 2020, too.)

But it wasn't *all* so bleak. When "social distancing" became a thing, my parents and I would take drives out around the rez, where we'd visit with family outside—from a safe distance.

Returning to my community was healing. If Native people are good at one thing, it's finding humour and light in even the darkest of times. My cousins provided me with some of the heartiest laughs I've ever had in my life, and I needed that desperately.

At the beginning of 2020, it felt like the world was ending. I felt like everything I had worked for—moving to New York, getting to *Vogue*, finally writing about issues that were important and personal to me—was all for nothing. Sure, I still *had* my job: I was fortunate that being a digital writer meant that I could work from anywhere. But I was scared that the magazine would soon shut down, or that I would be laid off. These were unprecedented times, after all, but I was lucky enough to have a job, especially considering there were many others who weren't as fortunate.

But, as the months went by, the *Vogue* team adapted. Over Zoom, the fashion team would meet every morning, trying to find inspiring stories to uplift our readers during such dark times. I profiled designers who were putting their sewing skills to use by designing personal protective equipment for healthcare workers, and interviewed celebrities about the art of dressing up at home, with nowhere to go—something I think we all did to remain somewhat sane. In a way, work was a welcome distraction, as it provided an outlet for me to connect with humans all around the world during a time where we all longed for interaction.

Then, in the summer of 2020, a cultural movement ignited. When George Floyd—a forty-six-year-old Black man—was murdered by police officer Derek Chauvin in the United States, the Black Lives Matter (BLM) movement swept across the globe—putting a crucial spotlight on the injustice, violence, and racism that the Black community has endured (and continues to endure). The movement brought to life some much-needed change in many different industries, *including* the fashion world.

At many different fashion organizations—whether it was brands, stores, modelling agencies, or magazines—a conversation about a lack of inclusivity and diversity began to take place. For too long, fashion had clearly prioritized only white faces and voices, and the BLM movement called for a broader cultural awakening. This felt like an overdue call to action: fashion designers, after all, loved to celebrate different cultures all around the world, drawing inspiration from them for their own designs (often without credit).

It soon became clear that *Vogue* had a duty to become more inclusive around who we featured, too. In my own work, I wanted to put a bigger focus on profiling designers who were honouring their culture through style. In addition to the Indigenous designers I had previously profiled, I now began writing about designers from all different backgrounds, from Filipino to West African to Chinese. I began to see how the fashion world was, slowly, vowing to become a more inclusive space. It was something I had hoped to see since I was a little rez kid who never saw himself in the pages of magazines.

It didn't take long to see the positive ripple effects. By the next year, fashion—at least to me—seemed like a dramatically more welcoming space. Sure, it still wasn't a perfect place by any means, but finally seeing a variety of cultures, perspectives, and body shapes in the industry felt, well, *refreshing*. I felt reinvigorated and excited about fashion again.

By the time I moved back to New York in the summer of 2021—when COVID restrictions finally lifted and borders opened up—fashion seemed like an entirely different landscape to work in. Now, the covers of publications such as *Vogue México* included Indigenous models like Quannah Chasinghorse—an Oglala Lakota and Gwich'in supermodel who was taking the world by storm. Hell, in Hollywood, we now had shows like *Reservation Dogs*, with whole Indigenous casts, now on mainstream *cable TV*!

I truly believe the BLM movement created positive changes for all those who identify as Black, Indigenous, or people of colour, including my own Indigenous community.

Yes, COVID-19 sucked in so many ways, and it definitely produced the worst years of our lives. It stole time we will never get back. But in a way, I was also thankful for this time. The pandemic and the social justice movement that happened during it created some necessary changes—almost like hitting a reset button on the whole planet. The world got just a little bit kinder, a little more compassionate, and much more aware. At least, I like to think it did.

My own perspective on life and work also totally shifted. Superficial things became less important to me. My circle of friends became much, much smaller. It may have taken a pandemic and a major social justice movement to make it happen, but, for me, something finally clicked. I felt like the Creator was telling me exactly what I needed to be doing, and what I needed to be focusing on. A sense of clarity overcame me.

When I touched down in Manhattan again, my creativity, vision, and focus were stronger than ever. I felt the way I had on the very first day I moved to the city—like I was an eager twenty-one-year-old, armed with nothing but a mission and some passion.

For so long, I'd wanted to introduce people to the beauty of Indigenous culture and fashion. And now, for the first time, it felt like people were finally ready to listen.

CHAPTER 13

AANJI NAKE-BMOSEYAN
(CHANGING DIRECTIONS)

COMING BACK A YEAR AFTER I'd left, life in New York City felt very different.

Call it the post-COVID effect.

I felt a familiar comfort being back in the Big Apple—and a bit of foreignness, too. The city had certainly changed a lot since I had left. Some of my favourite haunts had closed down during the pandemic. I mourned Fedora, a quaint West Village restaurant that *always* had a wait (a worthwhile one); and Lucky Strike, the perfect SoHo spot to grab a quick martini (or two, or three) with friends; or Therapy, the iconic Hell's Kitchen gay bar/club where I spent many evening dancing the night away (among other things).

I mourned all of these defunct spots mostly because they represented so many fun memories from my roaring twenties in the city. It felt like a little piece of me—and pre-COVID life—died with them. I was beginning to sound like one of those old-school New Yorkers who say things like "*Back in my day, I remember when. . . .*" I missed the New York that I had known when I first moved there. I missed that chaotic spark it once had. The city now felt a whole lot less crowded—and that's because it *was* less crowded. So many folks had left the city, and many of my own friends had made big decisions to move away, including two of my best friends, Dianne and Jasmine.

The city may have felt different, but I was different, too. I certainly had different priorities. In my twenties, I'd been trying to carve out my own space in the world. New York was the playground where I'd worked hard and played harder, all in the quest to figure out who I was. But now, in my thirties, after spending so many months back at home in Nipissing, with nothing but time to reflect, I felt more sure of myself. My friend circle got smaller. I valued going out to party less and less. My career trajectory felt more laser-focused. At *Vogue*, I was now armed with a newfound passion to find and tell Indigenous stories in fashion. I also valued finding my Native community in the city, and going to events that fell in line with my interests.

The pandemic sucked—so much of it sucked—but sometimes, it takes a dramatic event to give your life some clarity and direction. I felt like a new person.

Suddenly, my Upper East Side studio—home for eight years—felt super crammed. Spending a year back at my parents' spacious house, with its huge, glorious backyard, made me realize just how inhumane New York City apartments really are. I needed a change. So, I did what so many New Yorkers do, and I moved to Brooklyn in the pursuit of space. That space turned out to be a gorgeous two-bedroom apartment with old-school charm—including a tiled lobby, crown moulding throughout the apartment, and Parisian-style parquet floors. *Honey, I was home.* I spent much of my first year back in the city decorating the space—scouring Brooklyn vintage stores for furniture pieces obsessively, like I was a professional decorator or something.

At *Vogue*, I was also getting back into the swing of working in an office again. The company took a new hybrid approach, meaning we only had to come into the office a few days a week. After working from home for so long, the concept of interacting with humans and commuting to an office building took some *adjusting to*. The days felt so *long*. But after a while, I began to appreciate the human interaction again. It stimulated ideas and helped ignite creativity. Well, at least for two or three days a week. I preferred my quieter writing days at home, working in solitude in my fancy new, well-decorated office. I felt so *adult*. Like I finally had my shit together.

At the height of the pandemic in 2020, the concept of living in New York again, and having a regular nine-to-five office job, felt impossible—as though it would never happen again. Yet here I was, getting back into my old life, trying to get back to a sense of normal.

But the idea of travelling still felt totally foreign. The pandemic was lingering, after all, and there were questions around whether or not it was safe to board an airplane. Then, suddenly, a travel opportunity arose.

A press release arrived in my inbox that immediately piqued my curiosity.

"This August, the Santa Fe Indian Market will be held IN-PERSON once again!"

I had attended Indian Market in Santa Fe once before, back in the summer of 2019. The annual market is *the event* for Indigenous fashion—the biggest and best of its kind in North America, and possibly the world. It's held every year in the city's historic main plaza downtown, and the affair sees Indigenous artists from across North America gather to sell and showcase their new works. This includes contemporary jewellers, potters, silversmiths, textile designers, clothing designers, painters, and so much more. Even better, the artists come from a variety of different nations and regions—representing a beautiful tapestry of backgrounds and stories.

Concluding Indian Market weekend, meanwhile, is the annual Indigenous Fashion Show, which serves as one of the event's main draws. On the catwalk, top Indigenous designers debut their new ready-to-wear and couture collections— all modelled by Indigenous models, no less. The event truly showcases Native design excellence. There are no stereotypical headdresses or buckskin dresses; these designs highlight the dynamic motifs that are found within Indian Country *today*.

I was thrilled to learn that the event would be occurring in person again. Its cancellation during the pandemic had left many Native artists in a very tough spot. Many artisans depend on the market for their yearly income. They work on pieces for months—if not the whole year—in preparation for market weekend.

Now that covering and spotlighting Indigenous fashion at *Vogue* had become my new passion project, the Indian Market seemed like the perfect place to find some exciting new talent.

There was no question about it: I simply had to go.

COME AUGUST, I touched down in Santa Fe and immediately felt a sense of eagerness and buzz.

Vogue had agreed to let me cover the Indian Market weekend for the website. Chioma had assigned me to two different tasks. My first would be to work with a local photographer, a cool-girl Indigenous photographer named Cheyenne, to document street style in and around the booths. People *dress up* for the market, and we wanted to capture some of the amazing outfits for our readers, many of whom are obsessed with perusing our street-style images. The second assignment was to report on the annual Indigenous Fashion Show, covering the different designers and creations that came down the catwalk. This one, I was particularly excited for.

But it wasn't just the work assignments I was looking forward to. I knew that many Indigenous artists who I admired—including several new friends who I had connected with via social media—would be in town for the weekend, and I was excited to mingle and hang out with all of them.

On my flight over, I couldn't believe that I was now travelling on assignment, for *Vogue,* for an event that I felt so passionately about. I had never dreamed that one day I would be spotlighting Indigenous fashion for such a prestigious magazine, and here I was, and somehow getting paid to do it. I was also feeling a lot of nerves about it: I knew I had to do a good job if I ever wanted to come back and report on it again.

My Uber picked me up at the Albuquerque airport, and as we made the one-hour drive up to Santa Fe, I was struck by how mountainy and *flat* New Mexico was. Driving past the rolling mountains gave me a dolly-zoom effect—as though they were getting bigger and closer, yet also farther and farther away. The desert landscape was unlike anything I had ever seen before. Back home in Nipissing, it's all forest and lakeside; here, it was dry and rocky. It suddenly made sense why so many nations from this area—the Pueblo, the Apache—made use of materials such as clay and stones; those materials were *everywhere* you looked. It was a drastic contrast to my own homelands.

In downtown Santa Fe, I stayed at the coolest little motel you've ever seen. It was called the El Rey Court. Originally built along the old Route 66, it was now a quaint, boutique-y spot that reflected its former motor inn roots. All the rooms had bright turquoise doors, and the interiors were decorated with graphic southwest rugs, exposed wooden beams, and cozy little fireplaces. In the middle of the grounds was a cute little pool with bistro tables and striped umbrellas strewn about. The whole place had a really chic, unpretentious vibe to it. Very Wes Anderson. Joan Didion would have loved it.

I checked in, and I threw my luggage in the room. There wasn't much time to settle in. The Indian Market's opening night gala was kicking off in just an hour, and I had to get changed. After all, the gala was *the* place to see and *be seen*.

Compared to fashion events back in the Big Apple, I felt a different kind of pressure to show up in a statement look for this gala. It had to be cute, but specifically *Native cute*. I decided to wear a traditional ribbon shirt that my mom and aunties had made me back home in Nipissing. It felt like a stylish yet traditional piece that would be perfect for the occasion. I finished it off with a beaded medallion that my sister had made for me. On it was imagery of a turtle, to represent Turtle Island, which is what many Indigenous people consider to be the earth—a body of water, with land built off a turtle's back.

I rolled up to the Santa Fe Convention Center right on time. The gala was already filled with people. I checked out the venue, which had gala-style tables arranged around the room, as well as a buffet and open bar. (We love an open bar.) I took in the crowd. I had never seen so many fabulous Native people *in one room* since, well, attending some of our summer powwows back home. People were totally decked *out*. Men wore tailored blazers or waistcoats with big, chunky turquoise squash blossoms and belts. Brimmed hats in tan suede gave certain looks a cool, dressy feel. Women wore printed gowns in various Indigenous prints—silky frocks printed with images of elk teeth, dentalium shells, or Ojibwe-style florals. It felt like an Indigenous Met Gala—or the damn Native Oscars or something.

Damn, we Native people can really dress, I thought.

"You made it!!"

I spun around and noticed who was calling out my name. It was Jamie Okuma and Lauren Good Day, two of the most prominent Indigenous designers on the contemporary fashion scene. (In fact, they were both set to show their new collections at the fashion show.) We had all become friends through Instagram—the modern-day way to make connections. In the small Native fashion world, *everyone knows everyone*, so it didn't take long for us to connect and become friendly, even if we had never quite met in person.

"You guys look *amazing*," I said, giving them each a hug. Both Jamie and Lauren were wearing their own designs— sprightly, colourful printed frocks, punctuated by mounds of dentalium shell jewellery that must have cost a small fortune. They looked like real boujee Natives—I was obsessed. The unofficial dress code of the gala, it seemed, was to embrace cultural pride. People wore their best head-to-toe Native outfits, and it looked better than any form of couture ever could, in my books.

We each grabbed a glass of champagne and mingled. I gave hugs to the models and jewellery designers that I followed and admired on Instagram. To my surprise, people also came up to me and told *me* how much they appreciated *my* work and writing—that I was bringing a fresh perspective to *Vogue*.

There was a real sense of community in the room—a feeling that I had longed to find in fashion for so much of my life. Only one hour in, and the gala already felt like a homecoming—a place for Indigenous creatives to gather, reconnect, and totally fangirl over one another. And unlike the first time I'd attended the market, back in 2019, I finally felt like I was dressed the part—standing just a little bit taller and more confident in my custom-made ribbon shirt.

THE NEXT MORNING was the official kickoff of Indian Market, which spans two full days. Crowds of patrons—all donning mandatory masks, of course!—were already browsing the outdoor booths, which lined the streets of the historic plaza square. Booth after booth: the sea of different artists was overwhelming at first glance, each with an array of treasures to be found. Turquoise jewellery! Handmade hide moccasins! Handwoven rugs! I was overstimulated.

This wasn't your average, cutesy little street market. At the gala the night before, I'd been told by multiple people to get to the market *bright and early*, as some artists completely sell out within the very first hour of opening. This was serious business. That's because serious art collectors—many of whom are insanely wealthy—travel from across the globe to the Indian Market to amass new pieces, whether it be a necklace adorned with precious stones or a Navajo Eye Dazzler rug that costs the price of a small car (and is worth every penny).

Though the turnout was nowhere near what the market drew pre-COVID, I was shocked at just how many people showed up. It was still clearly a big tourism draw for the city. Not only that, I was also in awe of the *outfits* people were donning for the occasion. Just like at the gala, market shoppers were sporting their best Indigenous-made pieces. Watching people walk around was like a fashion show in and of itself!

People were adorned with huge turquoise belts and rings. Their best ribbon skirts. Large dangling dentalium shell earrings. Men wore leather-brimmed hats trimmed with rope or raw hide. For many, market weekend wasn't just an opportunity to shop and meet artists; it was also an opportunity to display their finest wares and to rock their best Native fits, too. This was music to my ears, given that my task for the day was to document the best street style.

I met up with Cheyenne, the *Vogue* photographer, and we went around snapping photos of various outfits. We also got to know the people wearing them, asking where they were from and who they were wearing. While we were doing this, the market's annual clothing contest—in which participants model their finest powwow regalia for a jury of judges, who crown a winner based on craftsmanship and design—was happening on an outdoor stage nearby. On stage were the most beautiful jingle dresses I had ever seen. Men also wore voluminous, colourful grass-dancer outfits, complete with the large porcupine roach headpieces.

"*We have to photograph them,*" I said to Cheyenne, as we beelined it to the stage.

By late afternoon, Cheyenne and I had a real mixture of photographs—from teens wearing contemporary outfits like ripped jeans and beadwork necklaces to Elders donning their traditional outfits, like blouses made entirely out of Blue Bird flour bags. (*The* best flour to make Indian tacos; if you know, you know.) This dichotomy of the old and the new—the past and the present—felt extremely interesting to me. Mostly because it reflects where we're at in the Indigenous fashion scene *right now*. Designers and artists are constantly finding new ways to reinterpret the customs and traditions that their ancestors have perfected for centuries, and seeing this reflected in the street style—how different generations are putting the same things on their backs but styling them in totally different ways—felt harmonious with this energy. To me, it proved that Native design and culture is still very much alive. Not only alive but flourishing.

For the rest of the day, I decided to take a little "me" time—to shop the booths, that is.

I had a list in mind. In my messy little notepad, I had written down the names of all the Indigenous artists that I admired and followed on Instagram who had booths at the market. I wanted to visit them all. And so I did. There was Elias Jade Not Afraid, the Crow beadwork artist with a punk-rock attitude. At his booth, he showed me his new beaded skull and spiked bag, which quite literally dropped my jaw. At Keri Ataumbi's booth, the Kiowa jeweller showed me her new diamond necklaces and fur cuffs. A few booths down, Naiomi Glasses and her brother, Tyler Glasses, were showcasing the Navajo rugs that they'd spent many months hand-weaving on a loom.

The best part about the market was not just getting to see and touch these beautiful handmade works (though the window-shopping is next level)—it was getting to visit with the artists and learning about their inspirations, backgrounds, and creative processes. In doing so, any visitor will quickly learn that Indigenous fashion and design is not just one specific thing. We are a vast community of folks coming from many different nations, with many different techniques and styles. And emphasis on the word *style*: I ended up blowing about a week's worth of pay on some amazing jewellery pieces. Oops!

Later that night, I was invited for drinks at the Matador—a dingy dive bar that's pretty iconic as a go-to Indian Market hangout spot. My friends Claire and Inez, who were in town, would be joining. The Matador is the kind of place where you get beer or cheap drinks and that's it. The music and vibe changes depending on which night you go. One night, metal music is blaring to a crowd of intimidating, rough-and-tumble biker dudes. The next night, Top 40 hits are blaring as twenty-one-year-olds Snapchat each other. You never know what you'll get.

The bar was blasting eighties tunes that night and was packed with an eclectic crowd—though fashion-forward Native people were clearly dominating the space. In the room were different curators, artists, designers, models. If the gala was where you went to schmooze and be seen, the Matador was where you went to unwind and have some real fun. I spotted my friend Jamie, and she introduced me to a few more people, including a very prominent museum curator and a Hollywood producer.

To my right, a notable Native actor was casually sipping a beer, and I tried not to lose my shit.

I spent so much of my twenties going to raucous New York fashion parties, trying to fit in with some of the most vapid people I've ever met. But there, in Santa Fe, the cool crowd felt inspiring, and as I looked around the dark room—squinting past the flashing disco lights—I realized that I had finally found my people.

THE NEXT MORNING was the final day of Indian Market, and the day that the annual Indigenous Fashion Show would take place. This was the marquee event, and I was excited about attending. Six leading Native designers would be sending their new contemporary clothes down the catwalk: Lauren Good Day, Orlando Dugi, Pamela Baker, Jamie Okuma, Yolonda Skelton, and Lesley Hampton.

Of course, I was no stranger to glamorous fashion shows. I'd attended many New York Fashion Week shows for *Vogue*, including for the big fashion houses such as Ralph Lauren and Michael Kors. But this show felt different. Not only were these designers creating beautiful, handmade pieces, but their collections also had something that other luxury brands don't: a sense of cultural revitalization. Through fashion, these designers were all carrying forward their community's traditions and design values, and that, to me, was the most innovative thing about it all. It wasn't just a fashion show. Fashion was the medium, sure, but we were witnessing a reclamation. A statement that Indigenous people are still here, and we're still creating beautiful things.

I got to the venue early. The show was being held at the Santa Fe Convention Centre, and I wanted to make sure I had my seat. Given that I was covering it for *Vogue*, I wasn't surprised that I had the best seat in the house. A showrunner escorted me to a prime spot right at the end of the runway. I certainly felt like my outfit demanded a VIP seat. I was wearing an elk tooth–printed vest that my mom had cut and sewn for me, finished off with big wooden buttons, and a beaded bolo tie that my cousin made for me as a gift.

Guests started trickling in. Just like with the gala kickoff, everyone was dressed to the nines in their best Native looks. As I took in all of the outfits, it dawned on me that I was representing the biggest publication that had ever covered the Indian Market fashion show in its one-hundred-year-history. I'm not mentioning this to gloat or to be smug. If anything, I felt a sense of shame. I was annoyed, even—annoyed that it had taken this long for a mainstream fashion magazine to take interest in the show. This only meant that I had to do a good— no, great—job of covering it for the magazine.

As the front row began filling up, I took notice of a few prominent Native actors, including the dashing one I'd drunk beers with down at the Matador. A few Indigenous designers were also there, to show support for their fellow artists.

"Hi, Christian," a familiar voice said as someone took their seat next to me.

It was one of the senior editors at *Women's Wear Daily* in New York. We had met while I worked at *Footwear News* back in the day.

"Oh, hi," I said, surprised to see her there. "What are you doing here?!"

She told me she was covering the show for *WWD*. I was shocked. I guess *Vogue* wasn't the only publication smartening up and introducing their readers to Indian Market weekend. I have to admit, I felt threatened—not because I believed she would do a better job, but because I didn't want to get scooped. I wanted the big, fabulous Indian Market story first, and up until this moment, I had never had to compete for coverage. Now, it seemed I had a rival. *All right*, I thought. *Bring it on, bitch.*

All jokes aside, the truth is that I welcomed the competition and the additional coverage. In fact, I wish more fashion magazines would attend these shows, or write about Indigenous designers. It shouldn't be up to only one or two journalists or magazines. It was subtle, but it felt like a positive change.

On my other side, a stylist for one of the world's biggest pop stars—*like, mega*—took his seat beside me.

"Oh my god," I said, not playing it cool. "It's so nice to meet you. I am such a fan of your work."

The front row felt like a *real* front row—one you'd see in New York or Paris.

Suddenly, a hush settled over the room as the lights dimmed. The show was starting.

The steady beat of a powwow drum, mixed with electronic beats, opened the show for Navajo fashion designer Orlando Dugi. I had taken notice of his work the last time I'd attended Indian Market; Orlando specializes in creating intricate evening wear for both men and women—real fancy stuff, like fashion you'd see at the Oscars or something. On the catwalk, he sent down sheer organza gowns adorned with intricate beadwork, and a billowy white dress with an edgy caged bodice, revealing the form underneath. It felt like the perfect (and unexpected) way to open the show—defying any stereotypes or preconceived notions of what Indigenous fashion design should be.

Next up, formal evening wear designer Lesley Hampton showed an assortment of glitzy gowns. Veteran designer Pamela Baker—from British Columbia—showed velvety gowns and tailored overcoats that were stamped with West Coast–style crests. Ditto for Yolonda Skelton, who did these fun little mod dresses with fur accents. One after the other, each Indigenous designer had their own distinct vibe and flavour going on.

Jamie Okuma debuted a sheer, parfleche-style gown (which would later end up in the Met!) and a dentalium-trimmed blazer adorned with colourful ribbonwork. Lauren Good Day showcased her signature sprightly prints, which were applied onto everything from tracksuits to bags to breezy day dresses. The crowd went wild with applause.

The fashion show was clearly about so much more than the clothes. For one, modelling all of these new pieces was an entire cast of Indigenous models, representing different nations and tribes across North America. In the mix were even some up-and-coming Native actors, including D'Pharaoh Woon-A-Tai and Amber Midthunder. The casting choices were powerful. Representation for Indigenous models in the mainstream fashion industry may still be lacking—even today—but at the Santa Fe showcase, it was *entirely* Indigenous. It felt like a space for Native creatives to truly shine in the spotlight. An event for Natives *by* Natives.

After the show, I met the *Vogue* photographer Cheyenne backstage, to snap some photos of the various runway looks for my story. The scene was total chaos. Television camera crews were doing interviews with some of the designers and models. Photographers were taking pictures. Models were taking selfies with friends. I didn't know where to start. But after getting my bearings, I went into action mode—running up to different models in their avant-garde outfits and asking if we could take their picture.

"*This is for Vogue?*" screamed a young model in one of Jamie Okuma's beautiful dresses. She followed that with a squeal. "I'll do anything for you guys!"

It didn't take more than fifteen minutes for word to get out that *Vogue* was photographing looks backstage. Out of the corner of my eye, I saw some models discreetly putting their runway outfits back on, hoping that *Vogue* would ask to photograph them. Cheyenne and I got to work capturing a handful of looks from each designer's collection—making sure to highlight a variety of styles, colours, and silhouettes.

Simultaneously, I saw the *WWD* editor also getting a few quotes from the designers backstage, but I no longer felt threatened by her presence. She didn't appear to have a photographer with her, and I knew our photos would make the story shine. Besides, *I was writing an article for* Vogue. Who could do a better job than me?

"How was the show?" Chioma texted just as we wrapped shooting.

"You're going to *love* the photos," I replied proudly. "Filing the stories ASAP!"

The next day, I departed Santa Fe for New York. I spent the whole plane ride back writing my stories. I didn't want to waste a minute. I knew they would be great stories and great traffic-drivers for *Vogue* (and they were). But, more poignantly,

I realized the trip had turned out to be much more than an assignment. It had changed something inside of me.

I realized that the Creator must have put me on this earth to spotlight the breadth of talent and excellence happening within our community. I was brought here to use my talents to foster and uplift my people through my stories. I don't believe it's a coincidence that writing and storytelling is the only thing I've ever been good at. For the first time in, well, forever, I felt like I was exactly where I needed to be, and doing exactly what I was meant to be doing.

Attending Indian Market opened my eyes to a whole new world—a world in which Indigenous fashion has a platform to shine, and a world where Native creatives could gather and foster a real community. It felt like I'd found my long-lost home in fashion. And now, I could write about these spaces to ensure they continued to survive and grow for many years to come. I didn't feel like I was doing ground-breaking work, but it did feel important. Better yet, I felt like I had purpose again.

I also realized that it was an event that *Vogue*—and other fashion magazines, too—needed to cover every single year. My work and my life now had a clear focus, and covering Indian Market weekend that year was only the beginning.

I couldn't wait for what was next.

CHAPTER 14

SHKWAASEG GCHI-NANKIIWIN
(BIG FINALE)

THE FIRST MONDAY IN MAY.

It's a date that people in the fashion world know very well. It's the date that the Met Gala is held every year in New York City.

If you're unfamiliar with the fancy event, here's a primer: The Metropolitan Museum of Art hosts a star-studded gala every year in honour of its Costume Institute—the museum's exhibition space dedicated to the history of fashionable dress. The Met Gala, which is co-hosted by Anna Wintour and *Vogue*, serves as the museum's biggest fundraising event of the year— raising money for the Costume Institute's forthcoming exhibitions, programming, and displays. It's also one of the most-watched (and discussed) celebrity red carpet events in the world,

233

so much so that it's been dubbed the "Super Bowl of fashion." No matter the year or theme, megawatt stars always come prepared to turn heads, and to make serious fashion statements.

The Met Gala is the biggest fashion spectacle in the world, even more than the Oscars red carpet.

I've had the privilege of working four Met Galas since I started at *Vogue*. My first time, back in 2018, was for the "Heavenly Bodies" theme, where guests came dressed in their best Catholic-inspired wears. (It was the year Rihanna came dressed as a high-fashion pope.) At the time, I had just started freelancing at *Vogue* and was still earning a part-time salary—meaning, I was very much broke. I managed to scrounge up a black suit and white shirt and punctuated it with a polka-dotted Alexander McQueen bowtie that I'd bought for myself back in 2011—the year that McQueen was the theme of the Met Gala.

The second time I worked gala was in 2019, when the theme was "Camp." That gala saw guests hit the red carpet in their kitschiest, most over-the-top couture. (Think: lots of feathers, sequins, and a rainbow colour palette.) I wore a ruffled-neck white blouse with a black suit, feathered bag, and sequined Louboutin boots.

When I worked the Met Gala, I was not attending as a celebrity guest; I was in the museum's "war room," as we call it, where all of *Vogue*'s staff sits at computers and bangs out digital coverage of the red carpet. Even though I've always been far away from the red carpet itself, and from the stars mingling inside, I've never cared. It was exciting just to be in proximity to the action. You could *feel* the buzz and excitement among the staff, even as we were cranking out coverage.

My third Met Gala, in 2023, was a much different experience.

"I have some good news," Chioma told me as I sat down in her office for one of our regular pre–Met Gala meetings. "You're actually going to be on the red carpet this year at the Met."

"What?" I asked, temporarily stunned.

Being on the Met Gala red carpet was sort of like an urban legend: something people talked about but never quite achieved. Getting a press spot on the famous Met steps was notoriously hard—even as a *Vogue* employee. In the same way every celebrity in the world wants to score an invite to the gala, every journalist in fashion wants to earn a spot on that red carpet. It was a privilege I thought would take years to earn. But here I was, receiving the prestigious honour.

"You'll be spearheading *Vogue*'s Best Dressed list for the night," Chioma continued, "so you'll have a great red carpet spot to take in all of the looks as they arrive. Be sure to come dressed!"

I was totally in shock. I couldn't believe I would be just an arm's length away from so many A-listers, at one of the biggest fashion events *in the world*, no less. This year's theme, I learned, was honouring the work of the late designer Karl Lagerfeld—the iconic talent who had spearheaded the design vision at labels such as Chanel, Fendi, Chloé, and Balmain. I immediately started stressing about—what else?—what to wear. I knew that my outfit would have to honour Lagerfeld in some way or another.

This was my highest-stakes assignment to date. Sure, I had worked the Met before—and I knew how intense and fast-paced the night would be. But I had never been on the red carpet, and never with such an important task: I would be editing the list of the night's best-dressed stars—the celebrities that *Vogue* considers the most fashionable winners of the night. Met Gala red carpet fashion coverage is something that *Vogue* readers look forward to, and it's one of the most-read stories in the magazine for the whole year. So, you know, no pressure.

In the weeks leading up to the Met, the *Vogue* staff spent countless hours in meetings and preparing for the big night. We treated preparations for gala as seriously as government officials would for, say, the presidential inauguration. Every detail was meticulously planned out. The events team pored over the guest list, seating arrangements, floral arrangements, and dinner menu. The editorial team planned out which stories we'd publish in the big lead-up to the Met, who would be covering what, and who would post what when. Every detail was planned to perfection.

Closer to the night, the fashion team began to learn which celebrities would be attending, and what they would be wearing—information that's kept extremely confidential. "Apparently, one guest wants to come dressed as Choupette—Karl Lagerfeld's cat," Chioma told me during one of our weekly touch-bases. No inspiration or idea seemed too outlandish for the Met, and it was super exciting to know what the stars were wearing before anyone else.

At my desk—which, admittedly, feels dramatically cosmopolitan, looking out onto the Hudson River amid tall skyscrapers—I started pre-writing stories and planning my coverage for the night. I knew that *speed* would be the most important thing in the moment. I was thrilled to be able to write about certain red carpet looks before anyone else. Around the office, there was a palpable sense of energy, excitement, and stress in the air. For the magazine, in general, and for me, in particular, the Met Gala was always *the* most exciting time of year.

And this time, I had one of the event's most important jobs.

THE DAY OF the Met Gala arrived. I woke up at my apartment in Brooklyn at 5 a.m., unable to sleep, knowing what lay ahead. I was buzzing with anticipation—and major nerves.

Bright and early, I rode the subway to my friend Nikki's apartment in the Upper East Side, where I would be getting ready for the big night. Her place was just a quick five-minute car ride to the Met, and I figured getting ready there would minimize the risk of me arriving late. Schlepping uptown with my garment bag, jewellery, and shoes was a humbling experience—clearly, I was not an A-list star showing up in a fancy limousine or Escalade!—but I felt like one anyway. I beamed for the entire forty-five-minute commute.

I was on my way to the red carpet at the friggin' *Met*!

I asked two friends to do my glam for the red carpet. Sure, I wasn't *walking* the carpet like a celebrity, but given that I would be near them—and among hundreds of paparazzi cameras, which might document me in the background—I felt the need to step it up. One of those friends was Eiza, an Indigenous makeup artist I had met through Instagram; the other was Michaela, my hairstylist of almost a decade. I trusted both of them to make me look pretty. I wanted to look like I belonged.

"Are you nervous?" asked Eiza as she patted concealer under my eyes.

"Not really," I lied. "I'm just super excited!" I could feel butterflies in my stomach. Back on the rez, I had watched and admired many of the Met Gala red carpets over the years, especially during high school. Now, I would be on those very famous steps, right in the centre of the action. I couldn't believe it!

Once I was glammed and ready for the night, I slipped into my outfit. On loan to me for the night was a white suit by Tanner Fletcher—a cool emerging New York label—that was covered in black bows. I had seen the design on their website, and it instantly reminded me of Karl Lagerfeld, who loved a bow and *loved* a black-and-white combo. To my surprise, the designers agreed to let me wear it for the Met. It felt perfect for the night—bold enough to make my own fashion statement, yet sleek and professional enough to wear as a *Vogue* staff member.

With me in my full gala-worthy look, Nikki and I stepped outside of her apartment to snap some photos. There was nobody around on her quiet Upper East Side street. I struck a few poses on the sidewalk. "Hey!!" a doorman across the street yelled at us, proceeding to beckon us over.

It was a doorman Nikki knew from the block. "Wow, that suit is very cool," he said, taking my statement outfit in. He worked at one of those fancy apartment buildings that has a concierge and an elevator and a laundry room—a rarity in New York. "Saw you taking photos. Want to come inside and snap some *real* photos?"

That's the thing about New York City—people are much kinder than you think. All of a sudden, a strange doorman is in a squatting position, trying to capture your best angles while you strike a pose inside his chic lobby. "We got the shot," he said.

I thanked Nikki for letting me take over her apartment for the morning, and then I was off in an Uber, on my way to the Met Gala.

Me! At the Met!

As we crawled our way to the museum, I sat in a contorted horizontal position, trying my best not to wrinkle my all-white suit. At a stoplight, a taxi driver beside us noticed this and laughed.

You think I'm going to show up at the Met looking like a wrinkled mess?

The *Vogue* staff had a 3 p.m. call time for arrival, just a few hours before the red carpet, which was set to begin at 6 p.m. I arrived right on time, entering via a special staff entrance on the side of the museum. Among a sea of tourists in casual wear—graphic tees, shorts, flip-flops—I caught glimpses of the *Vogue* staff arriving out of cars in droves. Some wore dramatic ball gowns made of tulle, sequins, or silk. It was comical to take in the juxtaposition of casual tourists and *Vogue* staffers in black tie—in broad daylight. As I strolled in wearing my bowed white suit, several tourists stopped and took photos of me.

Did they think I was a star?

The Met Gala "war room" is where all of the action happens on the night. Tables and chairs were already lined with computers, ready for us to write and upload our stories throughout the event. Usually, this is where I would be stationed, but tonight, I would be on the red carpet, covering the fashions in real time.

When the time came, a group of my *Vogue* colleagues and I were shuffled through the museum—like rats through one of those test mazes—to our spots on the red carpet. The famous concrete steps in front of the Met had been transformed into a glitzy red carpet stage with a giant tent overtop. Barricades lined each side of the carpet, behind which the paparazzi and press were squashed together. Gaggles of security guards lingered at every corner of the tent: they weren't there only to safeguard the precious art inside, but also to protect the celebrity guests for the night.

Taking in the red carpet for the first time was totally surreal. While the gala is an event that's viewed across the entire world, the setting felt surprisingly small, intimate, and controlled. I couldn't believe I was one of the lucky few to be there. Outside, hundreds of Met Gala fans were already crowding the other side of Fifth Avenue, gawking and cheering for anyone and everyone who even remotely looked like they could be an arriving celebrity.

I arrived at my designated press spot, which was located at the very top of the steps. To my surprise, it was one of the best spots on the entire red carpet, giving me a bird's-eye view of all the action unfolding below me.

"Christian?"

I turned to the journalist stationed right next to me. Her name was Zoe. She worked at *Women's Wear Daily*, and I knew her from my *Footwear News* days. I hadn't seen her since I left that job years ago. We chatted for a bit. "You seem to be doing really well at *Vogue*," Zoe said. "Are you totally loving it?"

I took a moment to think about what my life would have looked like if I had stayed at *Footwear News*. If I'd stayed in a job that I so desperately hated—out of fear of losing a steady paycheque—and hadn't taken the risk to quit, I would never have gotten to work at *Vogue*. And I certainly would not have been stargazing on the red carpet at the Met Gala. Quitting was a bold move that, clearly, had paid off for me. I realized there and then that, sometimes, you have to take a giant leap of faith to get the things you want the most. At the time, the gamble may have seemed totally illogical and stupid. But the universe has a funny way of making sure you're exactly where you need to be.

"We're at the Met Gala," I finally replied. "*Of course* I'm loving it!"

A gaggle of screams across the street rose suddenly—and loudly. We had our first star sighting! It was precisely 6 p.m., and one of the first celebrity guests to arrive was the singer Dua Lipa, who was wearing possibly the biggest diamond necklace that I had ever seen. (It was, in fact, a new Tiffany diamond necklace, valued at over two hundred carats.) The blinding diamond was worth more than, well, my whole existence. I looked at it in amazement. *God, I love fashion*, I thought.

Next up, Doja Cat and Jared Leto both showed up dressed as cats—a campy nod to Choupette. The camera shutters and flash bulbs started going off rapidly—like machine guns. Paparazzi screamed the stars' names repeatedly. Keeping one's composure and not blinking every second in those conditions is a true talent. I watched as Doja Cat posed in a completely natural, elegant way. Everyone looked breathtaking.

Soon, a flurry of more stars began climbing the Met steps. Top actresses arrived in one-of-a-kind couture Chanel dresses that sparkled in the light (Nicole Kidman!). Daring musicians showed up covered in silver bodypaint (Lil Nas X!). The crowd went wild, screaming across the street. About an hour in, it became impossible to notice each star walking the red carpet; sometimes, there would be four or five posing at the same time.

Compared to taking in the glitzy red carpets at the Oscars or the Golden Globes, watching the Met Gala fashions come down the red carpet is a whole different kind of *fun*. It's clear the guests are there to take risks and deliver fashion fantasies; for them, it's an opportune time to deliver a *moment* and get the internet talking. That's the assignment when you score a Met Gala invite. There were no safe gowns or classic suits—all the looks packed a serious punch.

And I was living for every second of it.

AS MORE STARS walked the red carpet, I couldn't help but recall when I was younger, back on the rez, and I would force my parents or cousins to watch me perform my "fashion shows" or "walk the red carpet." I, of course, always imagined myself as some big-name celebrity on the other side of the barricades—but standing in the middle of the action at the Met, I couldn't believe that I was there. I had made it. I had made it to this world that, in my youth, seemed so enticing and yet so remote and unachievable. If I told the kid version of me that I would someday be at the Met Gala, in a high-fashion suit, rubbing elbows with famous folks, that kid would have probably combusted.

How did I get here? I kept thinking, as each new star popped up in front of me.

It's an inconceivable thought to many kids on the rez—being able to navigate these foreign worlds where the rich and famous play. For many, the thought of ever leaving the reservation seems implausible. Growing up in Nipissing, I certainly never thought I'd ever be able to make a life for myself in New York City.

Yet here I was, a simple kid from the rez, who somehow made it to the Met Gala. No, I didn't sneak my way into the carpet, or stumble in by accident. I had *earned* my entry; I had been invited to the event. I was *working* the gig.

There are reasons why I find this so hard to believe, even now. The fashion industry at large has not made it easy for rez kids to break in. It can sometimes feel like downward spiral; a lack of school funding and job opportunities on many reservations means Indigenous kids are less likely to score that first fancy internship or assistant job in the mainstream fashion world, which makes them less likely to score that first entry-level job, which makes it less likely for them to score that eventual dream job. There are still many systemic issues in fashion that prevent Indigenous kids, no matter how unique or smart, from overcoming the obstacles so they, too, can "make it."

But my presence on the Met Gala red carpet—and at *Vogue*—proves that anything is possible. It's possible for a hard-working kid with a dream and naive ambitions to break into the field and demand a seat at the table. I don't think of myself as a pioneer or trailblazer by any means; I'm just a kid who, through luck, timing, connections, and, hopefully, a little talent, too, was able to realize his dreams.

If I can get all the way from Nipissing to New York City with zero connections and only two suitcases, I believe that anyone can. The Creator clearly had a life plan laid out for me, and instilled into my brain an unlikely dream that would require me to defy many odds to achieve.

But I did it.

Somehow.

On the night of the Met, I didn't feel a tinge of imposter syndrome. It's a feeling I've experienced many times in my career—a sense that, at any moment, someone will realize my humble roots and turn their nose up at me, banishing me from fashion forever. But for once, as I watched my favourite celebrities strike poses among hundreds of camera flashes, I felt a strange sense that I had rarely experienced before.

I felt, for once, at home. Like I was exactly where I belonged.

Where I deserved to be.

WE WERE NOW on hour three of the red carpet, and I was starting to get dizzy from seeing so many incredible A-listers in one space. My feet, clad in my chic black heeled boots, were also starting to *ache*. Leaving to go to the restroom, or to grab an essential sip of water, was totally off the table; you'd lose your spot in the crowd. So I stood there for hours, dedicated, not wanting to miss a moment.

Then I spotted one of my people. Someone *Native*.

"Quannah!!" I yelled across the red carpet.

Quannah Chasinghorse is strikingly beautiful, her face bearing her traditional Gwich'in line tattoos, both on the chin and on the sides of her eyes. What I love most about her look is how she defies conventional standards of beauty, and the idea that models need to be "blank canvases."

Why be a blank canvas when you can stand out?

Apart from appearing on the cover of *Vogue México*,

Quannah has walked the runways for major labels such as Chanel, Prabal Gurung, and Chloé, and she's starred in several major fashion campaigns, too. Not only is Quannah becoming a celebrity on a mainstream level, she's also a *superstar* in the Native world. Why? Because she represents so many Native models who have not been able to break into the mainstream, and she represents *us*—Indigenous people—in a space like fashion that so scarcely gives us a voice or platform. Seeing her walk in a show like Chanel proves to any little rez girl that she is beautiful, too.

I wasn't surprised to see Quannah at the Met. She was one of the hottest models of the moment, after all, and top models are always a fixture on the Met steps. However, the significance of her presence—as in, her being one of the only Indigenous people there besides me—wasn't lost on me, either. After I screamed her name, Quannah whipped her head around and instantly spotted me.

"Oh my god!" she screamed, running over to my spot on the sidelines. I had met Quannah a few times—I had interviewed her for *Vogue* and caught up with her backstage at the Santa Fe Indian Market fashion show. We were also Instagram friends—something that so many of us Native creatives become. We shared a half-hug over the metal barricade.

"You look *amazing*," I said, taking in her pink tulle gown and beaded jewellery.

"So do you! I'm wearing Indigenous jewellery." She beamed, showing me the pink beaded choker, earrings, and arm cuffs she was wearing. She told me they were made by Sota Scowi Designs, and allowed me to take a closer look at the pieces.

"What a moment—wearing Indigenous jewellery at the Met," I said, admiring them. I then showed her *my* Indigenous jewellery—rings made by my friend, Keri Ataumbi.

Here we were, just two Indigenous folks chit-chatting about our love of jewellery, as we often did within our communities. (If Native folks love one thing, it's some jewellery—it could be an alien apocalypse, and we'd never leave behind our beadwork.) Only, this time, we were chit-chatting about jewellery at *the Met*, one of the most exclusive fashion events in the world. Taking a look around, I gathered rather quickly that we were probably the only Indigenous folks present.

We were two people who had managed to infiltrate the high-fashion world, a space that—historically—has not always been so welcoming to our people. I wondered if there would be a time when *several* Indigenous people might walk the Met Gala red carpet. I can think of so many Native designers who deserve opportunities to have their designs walk that step and repeat.

I'm certainly hopeful for that day soon. Even now, it feels as though we're at a real turning point in fashion. Representation for Indigenous people is slowly happening in all areas and industries—from fashion to food to Hollywood—and there's no shoving the Indians back into the cupboard.

The Indigenous takeover has already begun, and like it or not, there's simply no going back. We can't go back.

Quannah and I shared a knowing glance after taking a quick look back at the madness on the red carpet.

"I can't believe we're here," Quannah said, squeezing my arm as she prepared to do her final few poses on the carpet. It's something that I've said to myself so very often throughout my career. *I can't believe I'm here.*

As she floated off and made her way back onto the red carpet, striking her best supermodel poses for the paparazzi, I cheered her on like a soccer mom at her kid's game.

"Go Quannah!!" I felt so proud of her and her accomplishments. And, at the risk of being cringy, I was proud of myself, too.

"I can't believe we're here," I whispered to no one in particular.

EPILOGUE

I'VE ALWAYS FELT that Indigenous regalia is regal—the fanciest of the fanciest—so it's always surprised me that it's so rarely had a presence on mainstream red carpets. To me, our cultural beadwork and ribbonwork is just as dazzling as diamonds or sequins.

In May 2024, I got the chance to bring Native couture to such a space—the Met Gala, no less. It was my fourth time working the event, and I headed into it knowing I would need a strong fashion look. After all, I would once again be posted up in the media pit to watch A-list stars arrive in real time—and to get red carpet content for *Vogue*. Just being in their vicinity, I knew I needed to look *good*.

The year's theme was "Sleeping Beauties: Reawakening Fashion," in honour of the Met's exhibition of the same name. The new showcase centred on the idea of reviving historical garments that have been asleep, with many rooted in designs that reflect the beauty of the natural world (earth, water, flowers).

The red carpet dress code, meanwhile, was described as "The Garden of Time"—inspired by the J. G. Ballard short story of the same name—and encouraged guests to slip into their best nature-inspired looks.

I instantly knew that I had to wear an Indigenous design. Our fashions, after all, have always been rooted in the beautiful world around us. And I knew exactly which designer I wanted to wear, too.

A few months ahead of the Met Gala, I called up my dear friend Jamie Okuma, a Luiseño and Shoshone-Bannock fashion artist based on the La Jolla Indian Reservation in California. To wear one of her designs to the Met was, frankly, a pipe dream.

"I have a proposition for you," I said nervously. I knew Jamie was a busy and in-demand artist, and asking her to make something for little old me felt like a long shot. But that wasn't going to stop me. "Would you want to help me with my Met Gala outfit this year?"

Like me, Jamie was always hugely excited for the Met Gala, and she was already very familiar with the year's theme; she accepted the proposition with enthusiasm. Not even ten minutes later, we were already busy brainstorming outfit concepts.

Jamie, too, felt that Indigenous design was perfect for the occasion. She wanted to create a look that would represent my unique background as well as her own. "Between both of our tribes, florals are heavily represented," Jamie told me over the phone. It was true; in my Ojibwe culture, many of our beadworks and artworks are centred on floral imagery. And, it turns out, it was the same for her tribes, too.

"What are some of your favourite flowers?" she asked.

I thought long and hard about the flowers that I'd seen

around my homelands while growing up in Nipissing. Memories of purple lupines and red Indian paintbrushes instantly came to mind. These flowers also happened to be popular in Jamie's region. So a few days later, she sourced some photographs of these flowers taken around her reservation. She then applied them onto silk twill, and we landed on applying them onto a modern evening suit, utilizing a reverse-appliqué technique.

"With a lot of older [Indigenous] pieces, before they had access to sewing machines, it was done by hand in this reverse-appliqué technique," Jamie told me about midway through her design process. She was sending me photos along the way, building up excitement one snap at a time. Jamie utilized fine wool from England to create the suit. "It's a perfect theme to showcase contemporary Native fashion," she continued. "I love mixing the old with the new; it's what our people have always done."

As the blazer came to life step by step, I was excited to see Native couture slowly come to life along with it. It was all about the thoughtful details: the jacket was even lined with an original Okuma design, printed on silk satin. I loved seeing the process in real time. To me, Native design perfectly exemplifies "slow fashion," an art form where handmade items are infused with meaning and intention.

And it didn't end with the jacket, either.

Once the blazer was complete, Jamie and I brainstormed ideas for the suit trousers, which we felt also needed something special. (It is *the Met*, after all.) Jamie came up with a genius idea: What if we drew inspiration from traditional breechcloths, which have remained an integral part of dancers' regalia during powwow ceremonies? Nodding to the silhouette of a loin cloth,

Jamie added an asymmetrical panel on top of black trousers, which were then adorned with crystals and ribbons. "I wanted a very *now* look of Ojibwe style," Jamie told me. "In a lot of archival images, Ojibwe men are wearing blazers with leggings and breechcloths."

With its intricate blazer *and* pants now completed, the finished suit was delivered a few weeks later. Just days before the gala, a giant box arrived at *Vogue*'s offices in New York City, addressed to me. I knew it was the Jamie Okuma. Before unboxing it, I was praying to myself that it would fit (though, knowing that Jamie had taken my measurements beforehand, I had no real doubt that it would; she's a master).

I brought the giant box with me to the Ace Hotel in Brooklyn after work, where I was meeting a few of my Indigenous friends for drinks. I kept the suit packed up so we could all unbox it together. Obviously, they wanted to see the completed design as well.

As I open up the large box in one of their hotel rooms, we all let out a collective gasp. The suit was just as good as I'd imagined it. Better. And it fit to perfection.

"Damn!" they all said. "It's giving Boujee Native!"

There was also a surprise included in the box.

In keeping with the theme of "Sleeping Beauties," Jamie had wanted to bring a piece of history back into the present for the Met Gala, and she decided to do so by secretly sourcing an antique beaded bag for the look.

She ended up coming across an Ojibwe-style, fully beaded floral bandolier bag covered in antique Venetian beads; she estimated it to be from the turn of the century. "I love the colours of the glass [beads]," she told me later. "They're the real deal because they were hand done. Now, it's all machines. There's no humanness in it." To make it feel more contemporary, she added custom ribbon straps, adorned with Swarovski crystals and ribbons to match the pants. "With the theme of reawakening, it made sense to breathe new life into this bag," she said. It was the perfect mix of the old and the new—and a total surprise to me.

A few days later, it was finally Met Monday. I pulled up to the museum in the early afternoon for my work duties, dressed impeccably in my custom Jamie Okuma suit and bag. As the red carpet started and I took my place at the very top of the Met steps (the best vantage point for seeing the stars arrive), I felt proud to be wearing such a Native couture look. The bag, in particular, evoked a real wave of emotions; it felt as though I was holding a piece of history in my hands—like I was quite literally carrying my ancestors, and a piece of my culture, with me. I was. It felt poignant to wear an Indigenous designer to an event like the Met Gala, where Native talents so rarely get their due. Though that year, Indigenous stars such as Lily Gladstone and Quannah Chasinghorse made the community proud, too.

Who would have ever thought I could be a part of such a Native fashion takeover? Today, the Jamie Okuma design hangs in my closet, kept safe in a garment bag. I often wonder if I will ever be able to top that outfit.

But there's always the next Met.

ACKNOWLEDGEMENTS

THERE ARE MANY people I would like to thank for making this book come to life.

I would first like to thank my editor, Janice Zawerbny, at HarperCollins. Miigwetch for helping shape this book into what it is and for always believing in my story. Thank you to the powerhouse writer Michelle Good for introducing us. And thank you Jamie Okuma for letting me use your beautiful bead-work on the cover.

My parents, Peter and Nancy: thank you for endlessly supporting my ambitions and championing me every step of the way. I would not be here without you both.

My close circle of friends (you know who you are!): thank you for constantly providing light in my life, and for encouraging me to keep going whenever I doubted myself.

I want to extend my deepest gratitude to June Commanda—a residential school survivor and esteemed Elder in our Nipissing community. Miigwetch for your help in translating some words for this book into our Ojibwe language; your dedication to revitalizing language, preserving culture, and teaching our youth is invaluable. Similarly, thank you to my sister, Alysha Allaire, as well as Nishnaabemwin Bemwidood, for also helping with the Ojibwe translations. Your respect and love for our language do not go unnoticed.

Thank you to everyone who took a chance on me throughout my professional journey—especially Mosha and Chioma, two of my biggest work mentors.

Lastly, miigwetch to the Creator—for always making it clear exactly where I should be and what I should be doing. Your guidance continues to inform my journey.